THE LAMP AND THE LUTE

THE LAMP
AND
THE LUTE

Studies in Seven Authors

Bonamy Dobrée

Second Edition

FRANK CASS AND CO LTD
LONDON

This edition published by
Frank Cass and Co Ltd
10 Woburn Walk London WC1
by arrangement with Oxford University Press

First published 1929
Second edition 1964

Printed by Thomas Nelson (Printers) Ltd
London ann Edinburgh

To Herbert Read

2

*I assume that you and I can think we say
what we mean.*

3

*I assume that you and I can understand
what we think somebody or something means.*

MICHAEL NEO PALEOLOGUS

His Grammar

ACKNOWLEDGEMENTS

For this second edition the author wishes to thank the editors and proprietors of *The Sewanee Review* and *The Listener* for permission to reprint the following articles which for the most part remain as they originally appeared in these journals :–

The Confidential Clerk (*The Sewanee Review*, Winter 1954)
The Elder Statesman (*The Sewanee Review*, Winter 1959)
Durrell's Alexandrian Series (*The Sewanee Review*, Winter 1961)
Rudyard Kipling : a New Aspect. (*The Listener*, June 1952)

PREFACE TO FIRST EDITION

THE first of these studies in literary material was written for a lecture delivered in London and at Cambridge; the third appeared originally in *The Criterion*, to be included afterwards among series of lectures delivered in Cairo. They all exhibit, I fear, the defects inseparable from a collection of lectures, the main one being expansion of matter which can be more austerely stated in essays meant only to be read. Being designed as popular lectures, they are also something in the nature of introductions which may appear too simple to those already familiar with the subjects: for as that 'prince of lecturers', Faraday, re-marked, one should not give an audience credit for know-ing anything; and though in literature that is a dismal precept for both lecturer and listeners (and largely inapplic-able, since we all read, and all think about what we read), yet it is well to err on the side of being too instructive. They contain some of those generalizations into which one launches, which may be well enough to say, but which it is, perhaps, ill-advised to print. But I have left them on the whole as they were delivered, cutting out some, but not all the repetitions, thinking that to re-cast them might make them lose whatever spontaneity they possess. Their origin must excuse the frequent use of the first person singular.

Yet, though written at various times, they are all attempts at the same kind of criticism; and since I have freely borrowed my instruments, readers familiar with current writing of this sort will be aware how much of my general view I owe to Mr. T. S. Eliot, Mr. Herbert Read, and Mr. Ivor Richards. I here make them a general acknowledgement, as it would be tedious to point out my obligation on every opportunity, even if I were certain of avoiding omissions. In some places, with respect to special points, I am indebted to Mr. E. M. Forster and Mr. Richard Aldington. If it may seem that I have thieved too freely, I would plead that I am of my time, sharing in certain directions of thought, ready to accept anything from my contemporaries which guides me in the path I am groping along. Last, but not least, I am indebted to my wife, not only for helping me towards clarity and suggesting certain angles, but also, which is more important, for emphasizing the need of a direction.

B. D.

CAIRO, 1929.

PREFACE TO SECOND EDITION

ALL except the last of these essays, and the additions to two of them, were written over thirty years ago. Apart from a few corrections, I have left them as they were —even to retaining the present tense where the past is now appropriate—at the risk of their having a slight 'period' flavour. As, in a sense, they must have, representing as they do the views held of most of the authors by critical writers at that date.

Not that I have greatly altered my own views or assessments, though I may say, to avoid the slur of arrested development, that I have here and there modified them, though not enough to spur me to any change of my text. Lawrence died soon after my essay was written, having written nothing more. Mr. E. M. Forster has, to be sure, published other works; readers will know his *Abinger Harvest* and his enchanting biography, *Marianne Thornton*, all phrased in his old, delightful manner: but he has written no more fiction. Kipling did, however, publish one further volume of stories, with poems to correspond; and, since these reinforce a view of him I was coming to hold, but had not reached in 1927, I have added a talk I gave on the wireless in 1952. I rashly sub-titled this 'A New Aspect', unaware that this side of him, especially as regards healing, had already been more deeply and more widely treated by Dr. Joyce Tompkins in the January 1950 number of the *Modern Language Review*. I have a little modified this talk, to avoid repetitions, and, except in the first paragraph, to eliminate the first person; it remains, however, substantially the same as it appeared in *The Listener*.

With Mr. T. S. Eliot the case is different. The poetry and criticism about which I wrote more than thirty years ago looks different viewed through the perspective of the years which produced the tremendous achievement of *Four Quartets*, and of his later criticism; but I have thought it best to leave the impressions of the time as they were. Now, however, to his poetry and criticism there is to be added his dramatic writing. I have not attempted to consider this as a whole, but include two notices which appeared in *The Sewanee Review*. It will be appreciated that these record direct actions from seeing the plays before they were available for reading. Yet I do not find that pondering over them in print has to any great extent altered my impressions, except to give them an added richness. This seems to me to argue in favour of Mr. Eliot's craftsmanship as a writer for the theatre, of his sense of the stage; he makes his impact there, and not in the study alone.

Finally, I have added to this collection of essays one on a much younger writer, Mr. Lawrence Durrell, though I have considered only his four Alexandrian novels. A real study of him should include his poetry and his travel-books. Why I wrote about him was largely a matter of chance, of what it came to me to read, or was pressed upon me to write about. Whether he is more representative of the time than, say, Miss Compton-Burnett, Mr. Graham Greene, Mr. William Golding, or Sir Charles Snow, only time will tell. At all events he raises points of matter, treatment, and form, which seem to me to elicit considerable interest.

Bonamy Dobrée.

BLACKHEATH, 1963.

CONTENTS

INTRODUCTION

THE tendency of criticism to-day is away from one of pure aesthetic towards one of values. It is even stated that the critic of literature, however much he may desire to stick to art, is bound sooner or later to find himself stepping over his fence into the domain of ethics. I am not so sure. I am inclined to believe that delight may in itself be a positive value, the weight and workings of which in the domain of ethics it is impossible to determine. At all events, I do not feel myself competent to wander in the ethical domain, nor very desirous of doing so. The point of interest for me has been to determine what the work of various writers is about, namely what it is that has troubled their minds enough to impel them insistently to write of it. This might, in the old days, when criticism concerned itself with morals, have been called their message, but the idea of a message is somewhat discredited these days. Yet the idea can be made respectable if we refer to their 'attitude towards life', or their 'sense of values'. But since this is not arrived at by reasoning alone, the word I prefer to use throughout these studies is 'intuition'.

By intuition I do not mean anything mystic or marvellous; I do not wish to have any truck with a fourth dimension, or a sixth sense, nor do I wish to dally with any doctrine of inspiration. By intuition I mean merely the recognition that a thing is so, and not otherwise. In its simplest form, for instance noting that this table is bigger than that chair, and nearer to me, it is of little use to the artist, though of great value to the scientist. But

the intuition with which we are concerned, though it is
still an observation of relations (since we are not interested
in the isolated thing) only begins where the senses alone
are not enough to determine the relations. This sort of
intuition needs previous experience and thought. The
myth of Newton having gravity revealed to him by the fall
of an apple, or of Archimedes discovering the principle of
specific gravity in his bath, are excellent examples of
intuition. The scientist, just as much as the poet, is, to
quote Mr. Herbert Read on the latter, 'only capable of
his intuitive experiences so long as he receives some sort
of sanction from the procedure of thought.' Spinoza may
help us towards a definition. In the *Ethics* he remarks, 'I
call that an adequate cause of which the effect can by itself
be seen clearly and distinctly. I call that cause inadequate
or partial of which the effect cannot be perceived by itself.'
An intuition might be called an 'adequate idea'.

According to Descartes, intuition was the vision of an
'unclouded and attentive mind', but where the creator is
concerned, I do not think this is quite enough. We call
an intuition something which comes with the peculiar force
of a sudden discovery, almost as a revelation. But it is,
with hardly any doubt, the result of thought, probably
largely subconscious. That is the way we can distinguish
between a useful intuition and a blind faith, between the
vision of an unclouded and attentive mind, and the substance of things hoped for.

An intuition, then, is a sudden realization, accompanied
by excitement (so I think), of some relation: 'By Jove!
things are like that!' But a writer, unless he is a scientist,
is also concerned with emotions, his own as well as other
peoples'. But intuition is of objective things, therefore an
emotion is of no use until it has been objectified. This is
where poetry comes in. The need of the poet, to adopt
an idea of Mr. Eliot's, is to find some object, or arrange-

ment of objects, correlative with his emotions.[1]   The
relations between such things constitutes imagination—
just like Newton's—but in poetry it becomes metaphor:
in the drama it becomes plot, the invention of relevant
situations: in the novel it is more mixed, and involves
character.

I think further that it is only in certain states of
receptivity that we are capable of an intuition, of grasping
some fact or relation so that it has the peculiar force of a
revelation.   It is one of the functions of a work of art to
produce that state, so that the fact or relation presented is
apprehended as an intuition.   Therefore the artist's job is
twofold: first to find the metaphor, situation, or even
object, correlative with his intuition; this is what we
might call matter: the second job is to put us into the
affective state in which we grasp the intuition as such; this
we can call manner: it is the vehicle of communication.
First the artist says, 'By Jove, things are like that!'   Then
he says, 'Look here, things are like this!'   And if he is a
successful artist, we in our turn say, 'By Jove, things are
like that!'   We also come to the state of seeing with an
unclouded and attentive mind.   That is why it is not the
end of comedy to make us laugh, nor that of tragedy to
make us cry.   It would appear that if we are too much
moved by the emotions, the intuition is clouded: we are
the prey of 'inadequate ideas'.

Let us go on for a moment to Ibsen, since he will
shortly come under discussion.   Can we see the work of
art arising out of the intuition?   Luckily yes, owing to
certain scraps of rough work that he left.   Here, for
instance, is the intuition for *A Doll's House*: 'There are
two kinds of spiritual law, two kinds of conscience, one in

---

[1] Compare Pater's 'On Style' in *Appreciations*: 'Some pre-existent adapta-
tion, between a relative, somewhere in the realm of thought—and its correlative
somewhere in the world of language' [1963].

a man, and another, altogether different, in women.' We know the symbols he used to present that intuition; we also know how he confused the issue. Again, he had a habit of writing a little poem to fix his mood before he wrote a play. Only one has been published, so far as I know, the one which preceded *The Master Builder*:

> They sat there, the two, in so cosy a house, through autumn and winter days. Then the house burned down. Everything lies in ruins. The two must grope among the ashes.
>
> For among them is hidden a jewel—a jewel that can never burn. And if they search faithfully, it may easily happen that he or she may find it.
>
> But even should they find it, the burnt-out two—find the precious unburnable jewel—never will she find her burnt faith, he never his burnt happiness.

Here, of course, we have not the bare statement of the intuition; it is, rather, the making objective of an emotion: it is metaphor, it is a poem. But the relation of that object to something else was partly there, and partly to come, for Ibsen was not a lyrical poet, except in a minor degree; he was a dramatist, and the complete thing came in *The Master Builder*.

We must take one more step. Intuition has also been defined as an 'immediate judgement'. This again, to borrow freely once more from Mr. Read, implies value. I do not want to go into this question here, as I am not at all clear about it in my mind. Mr. Read's solution, based on Professor Whitehead, is that there is 'a further process of a higher faculty, and there is at present no better way of describing it than by saying that it is the sudden perception of a pattern in life; the sudden realization of the fact that an organic event, of which we are a part, is in its turn the part of a greater unity, of a unity limited in time and space, formal and harmonious'. For him value lies in the recognition of a universal pattern. I am not at the moment prepared either to follow or to criticize (beyond saying

that I do not feel quite comfortable), but his definition
would at any rate seem to cover the values in Greek drama.
I merely raise the question of value because I want to stress
the point that all intuitions are not equal. The value of an
'immediate judgement' must depend upon the experience
and the power of the mind that makes it. Thus part of the
ultimate business of criticism is to discover, not only the
intuition, but the worth of the intuition, for the position
we give to a work of art must be based on value; the
other part is to discover how, and how well, the intuition
has been conveyed. In this book I have confined myself
mainly to the discovery of the intuition, now and again
branching off into comparative 'aesthetic' criticism, and
sometimes, for the sake of readers unfamiliar with my
subjects, taking in description a rest from analysis. I have
only very rarely attempted to judge the intuitive judgement.

I have also a hope that this book accomplishes, if only
by accident, something more than analysis, namely that it
represents the struggles of the time to find a balance at a
difficult phase. From Ibsen onwards, the writers treated
are living in a world which finds no security in Christianity,
or in any dogmatic faith. Each of them attempts his own
solution up to and partially including Mr. Eliot. He,
however, has returned to the faith. His is not an isolated
instance, but whether it is likely to become general it is
hard to say. It is possible to see his point of view, to
realize the benefit, even the necessity, for some such
return, without being able to share the position. Because
a sick man desires health, and sees the necessity for it, it
does not follow that he can attain it. Many, myself
included, are in the position of the sick man (though not
too unhappy about it, and by no means bed-ridden), and
moreover, are not prepared to pay the price our cure
would require. We would prefer to find health by other

means. The novelists treated—they have been treated as novelists only, though three of them are poets—have each tried their own way to health. These ways, however, must be individual ways; they cannot be general: an admission which will bring a smile to the faces of Mr. Eliot and those who are with him in the eternal search for assurance.

HENRIK IBSEN

WHEN we talk, loosely, of the 'material' a literary artist uses, we generally mean those aspects of the world around him which he embodies in his work. This is really to shelve the difficulty, for his material, more strictly speaking, consists of those elements in his intellectual and emotional make up which his bent impels, and his skill enables him, to turn to creative purpose. The detached morsels of the surrounding universe of which he treats are no more than symbols, figures of speech as it were: this appears most clearly, perhaps, in Jonson's comedy of humours. I shall later distinguish between these symbols and facts, and it will appear that facts are in effect less 'real', in the common acceptance of the word, than symbols, and act as distorting media.

An examination of Ibsen's material reveals this to consist of a small number of simple intuitions, not immediately arrived at, indeed only clarified after a great number of years. His early works may even be regarded as statements of a struggle to arrive at his material, his mental core; but the germ was always there, sometimes quite plainly expressed, but not yet completed, or brought into relief. 'People believe that I have changed my views in the course of time,' he once said. 'This is a great mistake. My development has, as a matter of fact, been absolutely consistent. I myself can distinctly follow and indicate the thread of its whole course—the unity of my ideas, and their gradual development.' This apparent poverty is not a derogatory criticism: on the contrary, such a simplifica-

tion is always a sign of the powerful artist, as with the
irony of Sophocles, the hatred of the forced and unnatural
of Molière, or the notion of solitude and betrayal of
Conrad. It is weakness, not poverty of material which
makes the lesser artist, such as wistfulness, an essentially
weak emotion, with Laforgue, who, though exquisite, is
minor. Much material nearly always means both weakness
and confusion, as may be illustrated by the many 'clever'
writers of any age and country, whom it would be invidious
to name, since those of past ages are forgotten, and those
of to-day are in the full flush of their triumph.

Ibsen's earliest plays are by no means negligible, but we
may ignore them for the moment to consider the first two
in which he seems to have felt the whole richness that was
in him, *Peer Gynt* and *Brand*. These dramatic poems are
visions of two opposed intellectual approaches to life. In
Peer Gynt we have life lived impulsively, without regard to
human obligations, and with a deliberate refusal to face the
great issues. *Brand*, on the other hand, is life lived
uncompromisingly, with complete devotion to an ideal of
duty; and in the logical development of each idea to end
in common failure, we get a glimpse of the great writer of
comedy along classical lines Ibsen nearly was: for it is
precisely the function of this comedy to pursue any single
idea to a ludicrous excess. But while this should always
be kept in mind when reading Ibsen, what begins to emerge
from these plays is two units of his material: in *Peer Gynt*
the passionate realization that every man has 'set at defiance
his life's design', as the Button-Moulder tells Peer, and in
Brand the sense that every man is striving for the impossible.
These two units combined might have brought Ibsen to the
state of easy, genial, acceptance which is the wisdom of
much classical comedy; but since Ibsen was not quite of
the stuff of which writers of classical comedy are made, he
never did combine these two units; in fact, he pro-

gressively separated them farther, till in his last plays he would almost seem to plead that but for some fatal compromise, or some insoluble element, the life's design would have been accomplished. In *When We Dead Awaken* this does actually seem to occur, but the mystic implications of the play are so great, that its analysis cannot here be attempted.

Take any of Ibsen's heroes or heroines, they have all missed being what they ought to be—Solness, Rosmer and Rebecca West, Borkman, Hjalmar Ekdal, Hedda Gabler, Ellida Wangel, and Alfred Allmers, all, for one reason or another, have failed to realize the plenitude of their natures. Either they have misunderstood themselves, or they have wrongly estimated the things external to themselves. Take the same people once more; we see that only a miracle can save or make them, and they all live as though they expected this miracle to occur, longing for something to happen that they feel must happen. These two units then are ultimately the same thing, but some obstinate element in Ibsen presented them as obverse and reverse sides of a medal, which could not therefore be seen at the same time.

There are three other main pieces of material, mental stuff, constantly recurring in Ibsen, all of them really implicit in *Brand* and *Peer Gynt*; the first the intuition of the prime importance of freedom of choice, as in *Emperor and Galilean*, *The Lady from the Sea*, and *A Doll's House*, the theme recurring in *The Wild Duck*: the second, the realization that where there is no love there is no understanding, as in *Little Eyolf*, *John Gabriel Borkman*: the third, the irresistible fascination of death, as in *Little Eyolf*, *The Master Builder*, *Rosmersholm*, *When We Dead Awaken*. Simple ideas, very simple ideas; they are the sort, as Lessing remarked, that appeal to genius; it is the strength with which they are felt that counts. With Ibsen they amounted almost to an obsession, and his material was extremely unmalleable.

If we now turn to the symbols he used to give flesh to his material, we find that once he had reached maturity, he used the objects of contemporary life. There is no especial weakness or virtue in this choice; its force merely depends upon how far the writer can visualize past history to give it the same quality of life as to-day, or, on the other hand, how well he can handle present day affairs to rid them of inessential, fugitive elements. He can write historical or modern drama as he will. The third possibility, the fantastic, involves symbolism at two removes, and this can only be satisfactorily achieved, even if then, by the greatest poets such as Shakespeare or Aeschylus. Great as Ibsen was, he was not quite of that rank, and he never repeated the experiment of the comparatively early dramatic verse poems, for *When We Dead Awaken*, strange as it is, cannot be classified under that head.

It is at this point that it should be made quite plain that Ibsen was not a 'problem' playwright in the sense that his plays provide texts for social reformers. His problems, such as they are, are the eternal ones without which art would be meaningless—the relation of man to the universe, and if you will, to himself or to God. The actual social events of his day, such as are portrayed in *The Doll's House*, to take the classic instance, were merely the symbols that offered themselves. His 'facts', to attack this question now, were the current ideas of his time—the emancipation of women, or the crude notions of heredity—and these, it will be admitted, were distorting media, for wherever they were used, they injured the validity of the symbol. Thus *The Doll's House* and *Ghosts*, once the most exciting of Ibsen's plays, are now the very ones most in danger of oblivion. They 'date' as we say, and this can bring us to another point, the question of realism.

The object of art being to formalize, there is always and

everywhere a tendency for art to develop independently along its own lines, and away from life: it becomes what we call artificial. Then, at intervals, the attempt is made to bring it back into direct contact with life, without losing the benefit of the latest acquired form. Sometimes this attempt leads to anarchy, and slipshod realism properly so called, where the distinction between art and life, so difficult to define, is lost sight of. To-day, for instance, we have Miss Gertrude Stein. With men who are primarily artists, however, and Ibsen was such, the attempt takes the form of selecting more and more significant symbols from life. Every artist is at bottom a realist in the sense that he seeks for an ever more primary reality, but when he has achieved completeness as an artist, the actualities he makes use of take upon themselves the proportion of symbols. Carelesssly and scornfully to dub Ibsen a realist, as if that disposed of him as an artist, is merely to be blind to his symbols, to treat them as realities: and the proof of his power to create the symbol lies in the fact that his plays for the more part, where he avoided what I have called fact, do not date.

What it is that makes a play date is worth a little attention. The phrase means, of course, that when we see a play we say to ourselves, 'This is very curious and interesting—but how merciful it is people do not behave like that now.' We do not dream of saying such a thing after seeing *Lear*, *Macbeth*, or *Phèdre*, because within the limits of the diurnal events we have to tackle, we do nowadays behave exactly like the people in those plays. And, of course, they are no longer people; they are symbols which correspond with our experience. If when we see a drama, however strange the situations may be, we say to ourselves 'Yes, that is exactly how I would feel', then the play does not date. Addison's *Cato*, for instance, we dismiss as out of date precisely because the feelings of the hero appear to us ridiculous. The play is not well enough written; the ideas are not adequate. This, so far, is not an analysis, it is only a definition.

If we try to examine in what exactly this good writing consists, we find that it depends—I speak with respect to this question of dating only—rather upon what the writer has refused himself than upon what he has taken; and the things he has refused himself are just those I have designated as 'facts'. These facts are, we find, those currents of ideas by which people try to control life, to explain it, or to escape from it. What is destructive of *Cato* for us is that the panacea of the period was a rather high-flown regard for the sanctity of institutions, to which we no longer pretend. Every generation has its own means of escape from the harshness of life: the late eighteenth century found it in what we call sentimentality; the Victorians found it in general rectitude, or sanctimonious agnosticism; the Edwardians and their immediate successors found a loophole in a better social scheme, and that is why the plays of Mr. Shaw and Mr. Galsworthy have already begun to date. Woe to the literary artist who allows himself to use these 'facts' instead of the symbols proper to his art; in other words, the business of the artist is with the metaphysical, not the moral problem. That is why Aeschylus and Sophocles are, or at least seem in translation to be, greater artists than Euripides, though the last named, apparently, had the same power in words; that is why Donne is perhaps a more permanent poet than Shelley.

Ibsen did not altogether escape the lure of the scientific 'facts' of his age; he was a little carried away by the current of thought of which Darwin and Weissmann were the leaders. Though in no sense a profound thinker, not at all a philosopher, or even a reader, or rather, perhaps, because he was none of these things, he was affected by the movements of his day. In social matters also, keenly sensitive to what was going on around him, we find him affected by Marx, Henry George, and the scattered revolutionary disturbances of his time. But where the artist in him really got to work, it submerged the moralist, as we see in part from the different drafts of various plays. The case is not uncommon, and we are conscious of the same thing happening with Molière in *Le Tartufe*. In that play, which seems to have begun as a castigation of hypocrisy, the hypocrite becomes a terrific, if Satanic, figure, and the comic butt is Orgon, the worthy man who allows himself to be deluded. The intuition has come during the process of writing. Unfortunately, Ibsen did not always purge himself of the impure artistic element; *Little Eyolf*, for instance, which deals almost entirely with the metaphysical problem, ends up somewhat lamely with the moral one, and this is even more strongly stressed in the final play than in the rough draft. From considering, I mean, of course, emotionally apprehending, the problems of free will, love, and understanding, and the fascination of death, we end up by considering the amelioration of the lot of poor fishermen's children. The reality of the symbols, namely, Alfred and Rita Allmers, is made invalid by the introduction of 'fact'. In the same way Ibsen ruined *Emperor or Galilean*, in the second part, by his conception of the Third Empire. This does not occur in *Hedda Gabler*, *The Master Builder*, *John Gabriel Borkman*, or *When We Dead Awaken*; there we are back again with the thread balls, the centreless onion, and the Button Moulder of *Peer Gynt*; only now, in the later work, we have the direct symbol instead of the symbol of a symbol.

It is then quite false to say that Ibsen was by nature a propagandist or problem playwright. What I imagine happened was this: Ibsen being a man of very vivid imagination, continually brooding upon life, as it is the business of the literary artist to do, was readily struck by the horror or grimness of certain situations. His powerful imagination further made him see himself in these situations, and his mind, since that was its bent, immediately dramatized the scene, and he saw, because he was able to feel, exactly how people might behave and talk under those conditions. After some early efforts, the symbols he found most convenient to use were those of the life he saw around him; it is only because he sometimes accepted as truths those things, in fact problematical, some of which every generation accepts as reality, that he came to be called a problem playwright.

Another point which one cannot yet, at this date, omit from any discussion of Ibsen, is his realism. I have already touched upon this, but some more remarks may be made here. He was, of course, neither more nor less realistic than any other good artist. What this accusation really means is that his work was too much like every-day life, that the spectator got no intuition, no vision of life, to vary the phrase, from his dramas. A very cursory examination will enable us to refute this statement, for, in fact, as two of his characters say, 'People don't do these things'—and this, strangely enough, was another accusation hurled at him simultaneously with that of realism. As a matter of ordinary fact people in daily life do not commonly do these things, but Ibsen's symbols *often* quite consistently do, since in their own particular world it is quite proper that they should. To complain that Ibsen's world is too dingy for art is another form of the same charge of realism, but this is again to judge art as though it were life. As police court facts Ibsen's plots are dreary enough, but the dramatic excitement their arrangement produces is in this way entirely left out of account. In *A Doll's House*, for instance, Norah desperately practising the tarantella when she is almost dead with dread is life raised to the power of art, as when in *The Wild Duck* Gina is lighting the lamps, and

Hjalmar says, 'And your hands are shaking, aren't they?' This is sheer dramatic invention, but not yet creation; which point may bring us to the subject of his technique.

The remarks one usually reads upon this aspect remind one of the epitaphs of undistinguished, but blameless men:

> He eliminated the First Act;
> He practised Economy;
> and
> Towards the end of a long and arduous life
> Abolished the soliloquy and the aside.

As for the aside, that was already becoming unfashionable, but it may become fashionable again; and the soliloquy has already made its triumphant reappearance in the works of the Expressionists, not to speak of Tchekov. These, in any case, are not changes in technique; they are merely the fluctuations of convention. A change of technique is a real originality. Edgar Poe, speaking of poetry, noticed that 'for centuries, no man, in verse, has ever done, or ever seemed to think of doing, an original thing. The fact is, that originality (unless in minds of very unusual force) is by no means a matter, as some suppose, of impulse or intuition. [He, of course, is not using 'intuition' in our sense.] In general, to be found it must be elaborately sought, and although a positive merit of the highest class, demands in its attainment less of invention than negation.'

It is not enough for art merely to invent new forms; the form itself must be compelled by the intuition, for 'every work of art', Coleridge justly said, 'must contain *within itself* the reason why it is so and not otherwise'. Thus if Ibsen at all changed the form of the drama, this must be described rather by his attitude to life than by any craftsmanship (since craftsmanship is largely self-criticism or negation), for technique and content cannot really be considered apart. It is not enough to say that he perfected the method of the French school of Scribe and Sardou, but it is perhaps something to say that he abolished the first act. The clue may at least be sought there. In the French school the first act took the place of the Elizabethan first three, that is to say, it was one of exposition to replace three of history; it was, indeed, history related, or at least history told in dialogue, instead of being history enacted before the spectators' eyes. Ibsen's achievement, however, was not one of form alone, but of feeling, for in eliminating the first act, his exposition, or past history, was made to run through the whole of his play, as in *John Gabriel Borkman*, *Little Eyolf*, or in a lesser degree, *An Enemy of the People*, to take examples almost at random. The question is, What was the intuition corresponding to this change of form?

It was, quite simply, a more than ordinary sense of time —not one that time is fleeting, which seems almost from the beginning to have been part of man's acute consciousness, and now seems to be fading—but a strong sense that the past is with us here and now. That appears a small, even an obvious thing; but originality, even at its greatest, is only a tiny addition to man's sense of himself. All of us, of course, realize intellectually that the past is important only as it affects the present, but with Ibsen this amounted to a vivid perception, a devastating clairvoyance; he could not rid himself of the idea. Almost every one of his plays might be called *Ghosts*; and, by the way, since we have mentioned that play, this sense of his accounts for his curious predilection for the current notions of heredity. How strong a dramatic element this sense of time became is perhaps best illustrated by *Little Eyolf* and *Rosmersholm*, in which we get a sense of living somehow beyond time, so much has the past mingled with the present, so much does the future seem to be with us here and now. I venture to think that this is his real contribution to dramatic tradition.

Tradition, perhaps that is a mis-statement, for among all the so-called descendants of Ibsen—the Hauptmans and Sudermans and Brieux, not to involve the English imitators, I can find no trace of this; all these successors have copied the wrong thing, the crude thing, and only in Signor Pirandello, especially in his *Henry IV*, can I see any real traces of succession.

As to his general method, it is most easily described as classical, though I do not here wish to make any formal antithesis to romanticism. He is classical in the general line and movement of his later plays, in the way in which he manipulates his excitements, and orders our emotions to the end he wishes. In this he is not very different from, say, Racine. He is classical also in his economy and restraint: nothing superfluous to his purpose is allowed to exist. Try, for instance, to abstract from *John Gabriel Borkman*, which I am inclined to regard as his masterpiece, any one small passage, or even phrase; you will obliterate some essential piece of knowledge, lose some implication, banish some necessary turn of emotion, in short, seriously injure the play. But he is at his most classical in his treatment of his tragic heroes or heroines, and here the parallel I would wish to draw is one, not with Euripides, as has been done in Germany to the length of a whole volume, but with Sophocles. Take Œdipus, Antigone, Electra, and then take Hedda Gabler, the Rosmers, the Allmers—any of the Borkman family, and see how in every case, with both dramatists, these people have shorn from them one by one every support in life; how, piece by piece, every shred of hope is taken from them, until there is nothing left between them and the universe. The only question with which they are faced is the metaphysical one—What is the value of existence?

There is, however, a real distinction between the characters of Ibsen and those of Sophocles. 'All the heroes

and heroines of Ibsen,' Signor Croce writes, 'are held in
bondage of expectancy, devoured by desire for the extraordinary, the intense, the sublime, the inconsequent;
contemptuous of idyllic felicity in any form or shape, or
modest virtue contented with its surroundings.' 'This
impetus towards the extraordinary and the sublime', he
says later, 'never moves or has satisfaction save as suicide,
that is to say as tragedy.' It corresponds with what once
existed in Ibsen himself. 'I had a burning desire for,' he
wrote to Carl Anker, 'I almost prayed for, a great sorrow
which might round out my existence and give life meaning.'
This is very different from the attitude of the persons in
Sophocles, whom only circumstances force from that very
felicity they so much desire, and Ibsen's persons seem so
much to despise. As a result, in Ibsen we sometimes have
a feeling that there is an 'emotion in excess of the facts'.
'People don't do such things' is a remark we feel to be
justified. This would be irrelevant if in Ibsen's world it
was quite clear that they did do these things, or necessary
that they should, but this is not *always* so, and it spoils, for
instance, *Hedda Gabler* and *The Wild Duck*. This was the
Northern romantic strain lurking in Ibsen, that dissatisfaction with the conditions of life which seems part and parcel
of peoples who live in countries where there is not enough
sun, a sense of the hostility of nature. 'We are creatures
of the earth after all,' Rita says; 'But something akin to the
sea and the heavens too, Rita,' Allmers answers. And
Ibsen does not seem to realize that the sea and the heavens,
and the stars also, are of the same elements as the earth, and
that the emotions which impel his people are not always
those of overfulness and superior will, but merely those of
emptiness and moral weakness.

And here we may isolate another piece of Ibsen's
material, which I forebore to mention with the others
because it seems to be made of different stuff, in that it is

not a piece of material he shares with any other writers, but which is peculiar to himself, and part of his Northern romanticism. I place it here because it seems to elucidate something in his characters, to be a part of their straining after the impossible, for every character a writer creates is to some extent a projection of his own personality. Characters, indeed, are but part-symbols out of which the whole symbol is made; they are not the object of the playwright; he does not try to create flesh and blood; he cannot; that is the business of nature. He uses flesh and blood to give body to his material, and that is why Aristotle was perfectly right when he said that 'In a play they do not act to portray characters; they include the characters for the sake of the action.' For the action is the main symbol of the poet's intuition. This element in Ibsen to which I now wish to refer is what may be described rather crudely as his mystic demonology, which is baldly stated in the Trolls of *Peer Gynt*, and developed to its utmost in *The Master Builder*, but which lurks in many other of his plays. What really, for instance, is behind the failure of the sculptor Rubeck in *When We Dead Awaken* to realize his life's design? What is, in sober truth, that Phantom which tells Brand that earth cannot use him more? Is this not really behind the singularly Russian question of man-God and God-man which makes the theme of *Emperor and Galilean*?—for the three helpers are the agents who determine Julian. Let us, however, examine this 'doctrine of spiritual possession' we might call it, as exhibited in *The Master Builder*.

You remember where Solness is explaining to Hilda Wangel how the fire came about in his wife's house—not from the crack in the chimney, but from a cupboard; and yet because he had seen the crack and not mended it, because he had willed a fire, a fire had come about. The dialogue is as follows:

Solness. Don't you agree with me, Hilda, that there exist special, chosen people, who have been endowed with the power and faculty of desiring a thing, craving for a long time, willing a thing—so persistently and so—so inexorably—that at last it has to happen? Don't you believe that?

Hilda. If that is so, we shall see, one of these days, whether *I* am one of the chosen.

Solness. It is not one's self alone that can do such great things. Oh, no—the helpers and the servers—they must do their part too, if it is to be of any good. But they never come of themselves. One has to call upon them very persistently—inwardly, you understand.

Hilda. What are these helpers and servers?

Solness. Oh, we can talk about that some other time. For the present let us keep to this business of the fire.

Hilda. Don't you think the fire would have happened all the same—even without your wishing for it?

Solness. If the house had been old Knut Brovik's, it would never have burnt down so conveniently for him. I am sure of that; for he does not know how to call for the helpers—no, nor for the servers either. . . .

Hilda. Yes, but if it is all the work of these helpers and servers——?

Solness. Who called for the helpers and servers? It was I! And they came and obeyed my will.

This, it will justly be said, is not demoniac possession, but, as Solness tells Hilda later, the troll inside us that calls to the powers outside us, just as it had been the mere desire for the Troll princess that had made Peer Gynt father to a troll. It is, of course, in another form, the doctrine of the will, for when the struggle has cost Solness too much heart's blood, when he is exhausted, he is afraid the helpers and the servers will not come to his call. Again, later, he once more identifies the troll within with the devils without, and finally he states that it was God who gave the troll in him leave to lord it as he pleased, and bade the helpers be at hand to serve him day and night. All this was not mere picturesque imagery, for when we remember that Solness was largely a self-portrait, we cannot but see that in Ibsen the consciousness of power conceived of itself in this way. Though he might have classed it among 'the illusions by which we live', to him it was actual, to him it was an intuition, a part, according to our definition, of his material. But just because here the material is on a different plane from his other material, we have no cause to earmark the trolls as symbolic, and so solid a figure as Judge Brack, say, as real: Judge Brack is as much a symbol as the trolls; the material, the intuition he represents, is different and less peculiar, that is all.

There remains one very important consideration of which it is a little presumptuous in a foreigner to speak, and that is the language and phrasing of Ibsen's plays. To us it seems, perhaps, that the diction is a little too bare and austere, and Synge spoke of the 'joyless and pallid words of Ibsen and Zola'. But we have no right to speak of this, for poetry is a very elusive thing, injured in the translation, and every good play is a poem. Certainly Ibsen denied himself rhetoric, yet even this remark needs qualification. Take Borkman's apostrophe to the mines:

That blast is the breath of life to me. That blast comes to me like a greeting from subject spirits. I seem to touch them, the prisoned millions; I can see the veins of metal stretch out their winding, branching, luring arms to me. I saw them before my eyes like shivering shapes, that night, when I stood in the strong-room with the candle in my hand. You begged to be liberated, and I tried to free you. But my strength failed me; and the treasure sank back into the deep again. But I will whisper it to you here in the stillness of the night: I love you, unborn treasures, yearning for the light! I love you with all your shining train of power and glory! I love you, love you, love you!

But if rhetoric is rare with Ibsen, that other element of poetry, compression into a phrase of some deep implication, the summing up of some strong emotive idea, is very frequent with him from his earliest play to his last. One could fill a volume with such things, many of which are well known, like the 'Are you sure we should have gone after him' of *Little Eyolf*, or the 'Thousands of women have done it' of *A Doll's House*. A great eternal question is raised in *The Pretenders* when Skule says to Bishop Nicholas 'The right is Hakon's, bishop', and the latter answers, 'But by what right has Hakon the right, and not you?' just as a whole cycle of emotional life is summed up at the conclusion of *John Gabriel Borkman*, when the two sisters, at last reconciled over the corpse of Borkman in the snow, take hands and say, the one, 'We twin sisters—over him we have loved', and the other, 'We two shadows, over the dead man'. Here, indeed, we are reminded of Euripides, when he shows us that at the end of the Trojan war all that is left for the conqueror's emblem is the figure of the old and bowed Hecuba with the corpse of the child Astyanax in her arms.

If, to conclude, we try to fix the place of Ibsen in the history of literature, we can say that he belongs to the period when the question of the will was agitating Europe, of which the great prophet was, of course, Nietzsche, who, writing at almost the same time, broke himself against that something resistant to the will which seems to be inherent in life, and against which all Ibsen's characters shatter themselves. Indeed, is not the 'life's design', in Ibsen's sense of the phrase, in itself really just a function of the will? Is not the Gyntian ego the same as the Gyntian will? for Borkman had not will enough to call the spirits from the mines; Solness had, it is true, the will to climb the tower, but not to maintain himself there; Brand is crushed by an avalanche of snow. This surely is at bottom the problem of existence as it presented itself to Ibsen, the failure of the will to impose its own conditions. Let us refer once more to the comparatively early *Emperor and Galilean*, which even late in life he regarded as his greatest work, for the most of his own experience had gone into it. Let us recall the scene when the Voice speaks to him, and where having told Julian he must get the Empire, Julian asks:

> And by what way?
> *Voice.* By the way of freedom.
> *Julian.* Speak clearly. What is the way of freedom?
> *Voice.* The way of necessity.
> *Julian.* And by what power?
> *Voice.* By willing.

but the complication is added by the fact that Julian shall will what he must will. This scene seems to contain almost all Ibsen's intuitions; but this at least is clear. Whatever we may say of Ibsen, wherever we may place him in our hierarchy of great dramatists—but this is only a private concern, and not that of the critic—we shall always have to admit that he is a representative figure of a mode of thought that at one time was, and will be again as it has been before, very important in the history of our civilization.

THOMAS HARDY

THE popularity of which Thomas Hardy was the object at the time of his death is the most reassuring thing in the history of literature under democracy. There is nothing in his work to flatter the hopes and vanities of the great mass, as there is, we may say, in that of Mr. H. G. Wells; no escape into a fairyland such as is offered by Sir James Barrie; none of the abject sentimentalism which earns thousands of readers for authors who shall pass unnamed. Yet not certainly all at once, but after many years of labour, his austere presentation of life gained him, not only the highest honours, which after all were shared by so 'exclusive' an author as Henry James, but the homage of the multitude of readers, who flocked in their crowds to his funeral in Westminster Abbey. As far as can be judged he is sure of a permanent place among those who are sustained not by adepts but by 'broad rumour', though already, now and again, the voice of the incorrigible romantic is raised against him. Mr. Humbert Wolfe, for example, finds that 'Hardy has examined life and found it wanting, but wanting rather as an idiot is wanting, or as a toy designed by a malicious zany, signifying not nothing, but something with a faintly confused and malevolent purpose—like a very fat man in pumps aimlessly trampling a rose in the mud, and spattering his shoes and socks in the process'. It may be possible to deduce this view of life from Hardy's writings, but if that were all the vision he could invite us to share, gatherers to the show would be very few indeed.

There is, of course, no denying, nor any need to deny, that the thread of which the Wessex novels and poems are woven is a dark one of 'pessimism'; but what matters in art is not so much the name of the material, as its quality. Optimism is exactly on all fours with pessimism, romanticism with classicism, if all are equally shallow; there is, in actual life, nothing to choose between Micawber and the melancholy Jaques. Thus what it is that redeems Hardy is, almost obviously, the tragic richness of his pessimism, the humanity, the sympathy which he brings to it. To say tragic, is in itself to say something big, in defiance of all the journalistic abuses of the word. Though the great tragic writers throughout history can almost be counted on the fingers, and to put Hardy among them would be to presume upon posterity, it is by his relationship with them that he must be tried and condemned, or crowned.

The attitude common to all tragic writers may perhaps be defined by the remark of Gloucester in *Lear*, which Hardy quotes in his preface to *Tess*:

> As flies to wanton boys are we to the gods;
> They kill us for their sport:

but the great writer of tragedy manages to convey that though this be the truth, it is well that men should behave thus and thus ; that in spite of all the seeming cruelty and futility of existence, one way of life is better than another; that Orestes is right and Clytemnestra wrong, that Othello is fairer than Iago. Not that fault is to be imputed to the wrongdoer; he also is a pebble of fate, destined to play his part in the eternal drama of good and evil. The end of tragedy, then, is to show the dignity of man for all his helpless littleness in face of the universe, for all his nullity under the blotting hand of time. Thus stark tragedy is no fitting thing for democracy to contemplate; if the many accept it, this means that there is some other attractive element in the work which palliates its uncompromising character, such as the lyricism in Tchekov, the melodrama in Shakespeare, the glory that was Greece. The question that arises therefore, is—What was this element in Hardy?

To say that such a palliative exists in him may or may not imply an adverse criticism; it may, for example, reside precisely in the quality of his pessimism, as it does in the quality of the pessimism in Shakespeare or in Sophocles. Pessimism may be judged good or bad according to the depth of acceptance in the person who feels it; it is good if the acceptance is profound. The great tragic writer 'says Yea' to life in every fibre of his being, however terrible, grim, or ghastly it may appear. Rebellion against life itself has never produced great art, for the great artist can, with Keats, see beauty in all things, even in the inexorable working out of the odds against man. 'Beauty is truth, truth beauty:' there are few indeed who can have a tragic perception of the truth, and yet say that whole-heartedly; but it can, I think, be claimed for Hardy that he had this power.

Every artist, it need hardly be said, has his own distinguishing flavour; but before going on to analyse what this is in Hardy, it may be as well to refer to some commonplace and very old notions about tragedy, namely, the conceptions of terror and pity first argued by Aristotle. Terror is not to be confused with horror; it is something more universal. We may feel horror at some particular deed, like the doing to death of Macduff's wife and children in *Macbeth*; like the murder of Agamemnon in the *Oresteia*. But terror is more general, and is due to the recognition that man is a victim in some vast scheme, that he is caught in a net; the Greeks saw him trapped in the meshes of Fate; Shakespeare largely in those of character, from which was derived the well-known clench, not wholly justified, 'character is destiny'. Pity is rather harder to

define; it is not sentimentality, it is not love; it is, perhaps, tinged with admiration, and the heroic tragedy of
Corneille and Dryden is excessively coloured with it.
After all, our pity goes to Orestes, not to Agamemnon, to
Othello rather than to Desdemona. We say 'Oh the pity
of it!' not because someone suffers, but because something
fine is bruised or broken. Without this sentiment of
something fine there can be no tragedy; that is, tragedy,
to come back to our first statement, implies the dignity
of man.

These general remarks have been made to enable us to
get nearer to Hardy; the paving stones may be crude, but
at least they make a way. Let us take first the element of
tragic terror in him, to see how it may be distinguished
from, say, those of Aeschylus and Shakespeare. In what
particular sort of web did it seem to Hardy that mankind
is caught? No one to-day can share the Attic conceptions,
nor the Elizabethan ones, especially as what the latter were
puzzles the acutest thinkers. Hardy's attitude was, as with
all great writers, essentially of his time, and the fatal web
in which he saw man entangled was that of man's own
consciousness of futility. Man suffers, man struggles;
Christianity gave him reasons for the suffering and the
struggle, and made them worth while; but when a man
comes no longer to believe in Christianity, the sufferings
to which he is subjected seem only the work of some
maleficent, or faintly sardonic, indifferent demon, informing the universe. To Hardy this sort of terror seemed a
completely modern product, which could not have been
until a new type of man was born into the world. We
come across his statement of it repeatedly in his more
powerful works, where this feeling was most operant; in
Tess, where we are told that Angel Clare 'became wonderfully free from the chronic melancholy which is taking
hold of the civilized races with the decline of belief in a

beneficent power'.   And in *The Return of the Native* we read
of Clym Yeobright that 'he already showed that thought is
a disease of flesh, and indirectly bore evidence that ideal
physical beauty is incompatible with emotional development, and a full recognition of the coil of things'.   In the
same channel Hardy suggests earlier that orthodox beauty
may have had its day, and that 'human souls may find
themselves in closer and closer harmony with external
things wearing a sombreness distasteful to our race when it
was young'.   Hardy's tragic net is essentially a product
of modernity.

And just as Hardy's sense of terror, his pessimism if you
like, is peculiar to him, so is his pity.   Pity, we have said,
must have a spice of admiration mingled with it, if it is to
have the tragic quality.   We get this in Hardy.   What,
after all, is the tragedy of *Jude the Obscure* but that Jude was
something too fine for his circumstances?   Or take again,
Tess.   The pity of Tess lies in the fact that she was too
delicate an instrument to carve crude life into a satisfactory
shape.   It was because of her sensitiveness, her integrity,
her purity (the sub-title of the book is 'A Pure Woman'),
that she was brought to ruin, not because she once, half-
unwittingly, committed a fault.   There is no commonplace
moral lesson in the book, no nonconformist, or for that
matter orthodox, sermonizing;   if anything, it is the crass
stupidity, the blind cruelty of the accepted moral order
which is arraigned.   She committed her crime, and came
to her miserable end, because, even when the bitter
compromise had been forced upon her, the bright flame of
her light-desiring spirit flickered up at the appropriate call.
Had she been as lumpish, as thick-skinned, as sensible shall
we say, as her mother, she would have found no difficulty
in adjusting herself, and would have avoided the physical
fatigues and the moral agonies she set herself to go through.
It is always fineness which brings about the crash of Hardy's

heroes and heroines, as it is fineness which impels Oedipus, Orestes, Hamlet, or Othello. But whereas in Shakespeare the fineness is always marred by a fatal flaw in character which brings about the disaster, with Hardy the fault usually lies in the wanton, unseeing motion of the universe, of the Immanent Will, full of sound and fury, let us take up the gauntlet, signifying nothing. It works in spite of itself, unconsciously, after the manner of an organism, as shown to us in *The Dynasts*:

> In the Foretime, even to the germ of Being
> Nothing appears of shape to indicate
> That cognizance has marshalled things terrene,
> Or will (such is my thinking) in my span.
> Rather they show that, like a knitter drowzed
> Whose fingers play in skilled unmindfulness,
> The Will has woven with an absent heed
> Since life first was; and ever will so weave.

Is Hardy then so un-Shakespearian? Is this much different from

> But thought's the slave of life, and life's time's fool;
> And time, which takes survey of all the world
> Must have a stop.

In Hardy it is usually the Will which does the harm, but not always. *The Mayor of Casterbridge*, for example, gives the picture of a man who fell by his own fault as much as by that of an unsentient creation; even if creation, and this is true of Shakespeare also, is ultimately responsible for making the character.

Hardy seems to have been forced into this positing of an unconscious Will by an inability to believe that any Being aware of what it was doing could have perpetrated so heartless a joke as the life we know, and he has, in fact, a poem to that effect which I might quote were we here concerned with his poetry. The sense of this is bitter enough in all conscience, and indeed there is no gainsaying the fact that to Hardy life appeared wickedly cruel, a series of hopes perpetually cheated, of aspirations continually mocked. But it is not like a fat man in pumps, because it is endued with a remote and solemn beauty; and beauty, which Mr. Wolfe does not realize, but which Hardy did, lies 'not in the thing, but in the thing symbolized'. And, moreover, he was symbolizing, not the Will, but the reactions of mankind in face of the Will.

Mr. Chesterton has suggested that Hardy's view of life was the distortion of the puritan spirit, wedded to pre-destination, baulked of its belief in hell. For Hardy, it can be seen, was not a Christian. Indeed it is difficult to see how a writer of tragedy can, at any rate while writing tragedy, be a Christian, since if there is redemption at the end, there can be no tragedy. For tragedy, at least since the Renaissance, is a vision not of divine justice, but of divine injustice, so far as the notion of justice is applicable to tragedy at all. It is a cry of protest. And in spite of his admirable, if bucolic comedy, it is as a writer of tragedy that Hardy is great, though it be domestic tragedy, that form it has taken nearly three hundred years to mature, which it has done, not in Hardy alone, but also in Ibsen. Thus it is by *Jude*, by *Tess*, by *The Return of the Native*, by *Far From the Madding Crowd*, and by *The Dynasts* that he will live, even if it be by *The Trumpet Major*, *The Woodlanders*, *Wessex Tales*, and *A Group of Noble Dames* that he has most charmed his readers.

None of this so far, we can see, makes for popularity, and the secret of his place in general favour resides possibly in the choice he has made of objects for his pity. And here we must slightly modify the statement that he does not flatter the vanity of the crowd. It is still true that he does not pander to the mob, but it is also true that his heroes do not differ in their circumstances from the average humbly placed man or woman. Any man might be Jude, any woman Tess, whereas few of us can start circumstanced like Lear or Lady Macbeth. Thus we can like ourselves into the characters, endow ourselves with the praiseworthy qualities they possess, attribute our failure not to our own weakness, but to the harshness of fate. This is a criticism which has to be made of his work; he seems a little to gratify the vanity of the weak, a sure road to popularity, one which Mr. Charlie Chaplin has trod with high success. It is a flaw in Hardy, but which he redeems, as Mr. Chaplin does not, by an aloofness, a sense of brooding, of detachment, foreign to the film actor. There is in the novelist a much higher complexity of art, a far profounder grasp of the way human beings work. The hopes which he touches so intimately are of the best; they have to do with endeavour, with longings for all things which are of good report; whereas the hopes which concern Mr. Chaplin are mostly superficial, and as often as not are no more than negative fears. A further comparison of two artists of such different calibre can serve no useful purpose; but there is still this to be said about Hardy, that however much he may make us feel this sense of personal merging with his characters, they are cut off from us, as good art is always cut off from life; his figures do not exist in our time, they live in a time of their own; their space also is less circumscribed than ours. As in all figures of great art, however solid they may be, there is something aerial and intangible about them. However intimately we may pity them, we do feel them in the end to be greater than ourselves; we may look after them, but cannot do them good.

Another criticism, not very easy to answer, is that made by Mr. E. M. Forster in his *Aspects of the Novel*; it is that in his books character is made too subservient to plot.

Hardy [he writes] seems to me essentially a poet, who conceives of his novels from an enormous height. They are to be tragedies, or tragi-comedies, they are to give out the sound of hammer-strokes as they proceed; in other words Hardy arranges events with emphasis on causality, the ground plan is a plot, and the characters are ordered to acquiesce in its regimentation. The fate above us, not the fate working through us—that is what is eminent and memorable in the Wessex novels. . . . In other words, the characters have been required to contribute too much to the plot; except in their rustic humours, their vitality has been impoverished, they have gone dry and thin.

Mr. Forster excepts *Tess*; he might have excepted *Far From the Madding Crowd*; but with regard to many of his books, notably, I think, *Two on a Tower*, the charge is true, and must either be accepted as valid or shown to be irrelevant.

It is, one sees, the old question as to whether Aristotle was right or wrong; the old fight for predominance between plot and character. Plot, it need not be insisted, is not merely story; it is the arrangement of the incidents of the story to produce a special effect; the arrangement, not only of the incidents, but of the feelings aroused in us by all sorts of considerations, passions, values, which have nothing to do with the story. Now everybody is agreed that a work of art, even the most rambling novel, is not the same thing as life; it is something like life, but what makes it distinct from life is its pattern. Character, unavoidably, is part of the pattern, but since art is not life, the pattern symbolizes something for the writer. It may, in the main, symbolize one of two things; either 'life is like that', or 'people are like that'. These statements are susceptible of almost infinite shades, but both plot and character are merely symbols. The question then arises, which is the more important symbol for tragedy, 'this is how things happen'? or 'this is what people are like'? Almost certainly, I think, the former, since the tragic writer is concerned with the littleness of man (even though his greatness in his littleness) in the face of unescapable odds.

Moreover, he aims at the universal. If we become interested in the person only, the plot merely expresses a particular truth; not 'this is how things happen', but, 'this is what happened to Smith'. Character, naturally, is necessary, since if the people do not live the pattern will not be like life, and so the symbol will be meaningless. 'Character gives us qualities,' Aristotle says, 'but it is in our actions, in what we do, that we are happy or the reverse.'

It is true that some of Hardy's books are distinctly bad; *The Hand of Ethelberta*, for instance, to add another to *Two on a Tower*; not bad, of course, in the sense of being shallow, mawkish, without construction or coherent thought, but through being wooden in language and creaking in movement. But I do not think that in those books the usual Hardeian plot is very intrusive, not half so much so as in the acknowledged masterpieces. The irony of circumstance is much more insistent in *The Return of the Native*, or in *Tess*. If some books are failures, it is due to a momentary lack of vitality, to some fault in pattern, which may involve deficiency in character. They are not bad because they attempt nothing; they are bad because they attempt too much, perhaps with unsuitable symbols.

And before going on to the work itself, it may be as well to say a word about irony, 'that dangerous figure' as Charles Lamb called it. It is dangerous because it is so easily cheap: it is often the mark of the second-rate author. It must be confessed that Hardy sometimes comes perilously near cheapness, but then so does even Sophocles, in *Philoctetes* for example. Irony is too easy a way of scoring an effect. But so long as it is made to appear the irony of fate, of a fate embedded in life itself and deeply accepted by the writer, it usually escapes cheapness. It is only when it involves a sneer at humanity that it is vulgar; any fool, any twopenny-ha'penny cynic can sneer at humanity. But this Hardy never does. Like all writers of any worth he respects humanity, even where he hates it. No one sneers who understands; and though to understand everything may not by any means be to forgive everything, to understand at least saves anybody from self-superiority and complacency. And moreover, Hardy's is a humane irony. He may have hated life, but he loved the people who lived it. Voltaire, on the other hand, who was often, though not always, a cheap ironist, loved life, but, so far as one can make out, disliked most of the people whom he met living it.

To give us 'the common sense of what men were and are' in relation to the net in which they are caught, Hardy (pardon the commonplace) developed nature as a character farther than any other writer. His descriptions are amazing, not only for bringing the very substance of the scene before our eyes, but for what they imply; they are never mere decoration, a sort of frieze thrown across the background, as they are in Scott, for instance. With Hardy the earth labours, suffers, and groans, is scarred with experience like any human being. The plot, the pattern, of *The Return of the Native* would not be what it is but for the character called Egdon Heath, which streaks the whole tale. The only thing comparable in literature, which I can recall, is the setting of *Wuthering Heights*. But even in that great masterpiece it is still partly a setting; it does not enter into the lives of Emily Brontë's characters quite in the same way as Edgon Heath does into those of Eustacia Vye and Mrs. Yeobright. No one who has read it can ever forget that astonishing first chapter where Egdon Heath is introduced to us; so much of the experience of the human race is crammed into it. The landscape really is part of the emotion; it is not literary fudge, as with, say, Mr. Compton Mackenzie. Listen to this from that author's *The Passionate Elopement*:

There were Columbines and Canterbury Bells and blue Bells of

Coventry and Lilies and Candy Goldilocks with Penny flowers or
White Sattin and Fair Maids of France and Fair Maids of Kent and
London Pride.

There was Herb of Grace and Rosemary and Lavender to pluck
and crush between your fingers, while someone rolled the jack
across the level green of the ground. In Spring there were Tulips
and Jacynths, Dames' Violets and Primroses, Cowslips of Jerusalem,
Daffodils and Pansies—and so it goes on for twice as long, a regular
index from a seedsman's catalogue, to—Good Night at Noon and
Flower de Luce, Golden Mouse-ear, Prince's Feathers, Pinks, and
red Damask Roses.

It was, as Mr. Mackenzie remarks, 'a very wonderful
garden indeed'; but what purpose it served in a novel
except to stun and bemuse the reader, or make him out of
breath should he read it aloud, it is difficult to imagine.

Let us now look at a piece of Meredith:

Golden lie the meadows: golden run the streams; red gold is
on the pine stems. The sun is coming down to earth, and walks the
fields and the waters.

The sun is coming down to earth, and the fields and the waters
shout to him in golden shouts. He comes, and his heralds run before
him, and touch the leaves of oaks and planes and beeches lucid
green. . . .

and so on. It is the dithyrambic intrusion of poetry into
the novel of the sort of poetry, moreover, which is better
done in verse form by Mr. Sacheverell Sitwell. It does
nothing to help us to see life steadily and see it whole, to
enter into the secret heart of life. Meredith is trying, like
some modern stage producers, to make his scenery do the
work which the actions and words of his characters ought
to be doing. Not that its lushness is necessarily against it.
Hardy too can be lush, as in *Tess*; but it is for a purpose;
it is part of Tess herself when she burgeons; she is merged
in it, and but for it she would not have become what she
did; it changes her as she is changed by contact with other
personalities. I refer to the description made little by little

4

in one of the chapters set in the valley of the Froom; but
as it is made little by little it is easier to instance how the
weather itself alters the effect Tess makes.

Or perhaps the summer fog was more general, and the meadows
lay like a white sea, out of which the scattered trees rose like
dangerous rocks.   Birds would soar through it into the upper
radiance, and hang in the wind sunning themselves, or alight on the
wet rails subdividing the mead, which now shone like glass rods.
Minute diamonds of moisture from the mist hung, too, upon Tess's
eyelashes, and drops upon her hair like seed pearls.   When the day
grew quite strong and commonplace, these dried off her; moreover Tess then lost her strange and etherial beauty; her teeth, lips,
and eyes scintillated in the sunbeams, and she was again the dazzlingly
fair dairymaid only who had to hold her own against the other
women of the world.

This is not just idle frilling, it has meaning. It conveys
that, in an earlier phrase, her features 'had changed from
those of a divinity who could confer bliss to those of a
being who craved it'.

But none of the descriptions in *Tess*, nor, I think, in any
other work, has the magisterial quality of that opening
chapter in *The Return of the Native*, which in itself gives the
effect of timelessness in change, which broods over human
life and makes our destinies at once significant and futile,
matters for tears, or for indifference. The book opens
ominously; the curtain is going up on a tragedy. There
is no blaring of trumpets, the words are subdued and
unpretentious; but the sound of them ushers in the drama
with a master's sureness of instrumentation:

A Saturday afternoon in November was approaching the time of
twilight, and the vast tract of unenclosed wild known as Egdon Heath
embrowned itself moment by moment.   Overhead the hollow
stretch of whitish cloud shutting out the sky was as a tent which
had the whole heath for its floor.

The chapter is a single unit which cannot really be retailed

in fragments; but since one must select, I would take the
last paragraph but one:

To recline on a stump of thorn in the central valley of Egdon,
between afternoon and night, as now, when the eye could reach
nothing of the world outside the summits and shoulders of heathland
which filled the whole circumference of its glance, and to know that
everything around and underneath had been from pre-historic times
as unaltered as the stars overhead, gave ballast to the mind adrift on
change, and harassed by the irrepressible New. The great inviolate
place had an ancient permanence which the sea cannot claim. Who
can say of a particular sea that it is old? Distilled by the sun,
kneaded by the moon, it is renewed in a year, in a day, in an hour.
The sea changed, the fields changed, the rivers, the villages and the
people changed, yet Egdon remained. Those surfaces were neither
so steep as to be destructible by weather, nor so flat as to be the
victims of floods and deposits. With the exception of an aged
highway, and a still more aged barrow presently to be referred to—
themselves almost crystallized to natural products by long continuance—even the trifling irregularities were not caused by pickaxe,
plough or spade, but remained as the very finger-touches of the last
geological change.

Now even at the risk of being tedious on this question
of scenery, there are still some things to be observed about
that chapter. The heath is not a token, like the volcano in
Conrad's *Victory*, or the silver mine in *Nostromo*, nor like
the lake in Tchekov's *The Seagull*. Nor is it valuable on
account of the sense of intimacy with nature, which we get
even more closely in some of his other novels, such as *The
Woodlanders*, and in which he does not equal, certainly does
not surpass Tolstoy in those superb hunting and shooting
scenes in *War and Peace* and *Anna Karenina*. Nor is it
merely that it gives us the sense of puny mortals acting out
their little drama of a moment against boundless time; it
is that Egdon Heath is itself a character, and acts on human
beings just as other humans do. Without it, not Eustacia
Vye, nor the Reddleman, nor Clym Yeobright, nor
Thomasin, nor even deaf, grotesque old Grandfer Cantle

would have been the same. In Hardy's novels it may not be fate that is shown working through us, but it is certainly the earth working through us, both the earth and ourselves being part of the expression of the Immanent Will, or, if you prefer, the blind Creative Principle.

The earth, then, is alive in Hardy; but what of his people? Is it true that, his bucolics apart, they are thinned to nothing? Let us be quite fair to Mr. Forster and leave out *Tess*. Is it true that they conform so much to the exigencies of the plot that they seem to lack volition, to be unendowed with

> All thoughts, all passions, all delights,
> Whatever stirs this mortal frame,

so that we do not seem to hear human voices speaking to us out of the silence we create around ourselves when we read, but only see puppets dangled by too obvious strings? Sometimes, yes, admittedly; even, perhaps, to add to the number, in *Jude the Obscure*. But it is not so, I venture to maintain, in *The Trumpet Major*, *Far From the Madding Crowd*, and *The Mayor of Casterbridge*, to name only three. I would add a fourth certain exception, but that some have found the ironic coincidences in *The Return of the Native* stretched too far, though such ironies are to be found in other writers. Cordelia died by the delay of a minute; had Desdemona dropped her handkerchief in any other place, or at any other time than she did, there would have been no tragedy of Othello. But think of any of the main character in the three books I have chosen; the events in all of them *seem* at least to flow out of the wilful acts of human beings. To take one example, there is no need for the Trumpet Major himself to have been so delicate, so scrupulous, with respect to his brother. Nor is there any thinness in the mayor, nor lack of blood in the delightful and touching heroine of *Far From the Madding Crowd*.

Characters which change and grow are not inhuman, however low they may bow to the bitter facts of life.

Moreover, in Hardy's work, we never lose the thread of a vein of humour, itself a pledge of life, which runs through it, something quite apart from his ironic humour, and usually coupled with his bucolics. That word inevitably arises when speaking of his peasants, since it has, in English, a faintly comic flavour, a tang of something laughable and broad, as well as rustic and homely. There is more than a hint of something gnome-like and eternal, very much of the earth, in such persons as Grandfer Cantle or Corporal Tullidge, not to mention that more striking, because peculiarly placed son of the soil, Sir John d'Urberville. The definitely comic stories are not so characteristic, because they are more traditional; they remind us of Fielding or Smollett. Take, for instance, that tale of the church band, who forgot themselves so disastrously one Sunday afternoon service, and fell asleep owing to over-junketing during the previous week, especially on the night before; among whom, waking up suddenly, the principal player imagined himself still at a frolic, and instead of tuning up into a solemn hymn, burst out into the liveliest country dance; and the rest, starting up from slumber, automatically followed his lead, till the church was filled with sounds so rollicking and gay, that only Satan himself could have prompted them. It is in the best English manner, full of sympathy, for the English have never despised their comic characters, except when the Comedy of Manners ruled the stage; we are proud of Falstaff, and like Bardolph, would be with him wheresoe'er he be whether in heaven or in hell. We love Uncle Toby and Sam Weller as the French despise Messieurs Bouvard and Pécuchet. But in the pieces that are most Hardyesque, there is, though still predominantly humorous, something slightly grim and more than grotesque, a reminder that though the earth is our mother, she is also our grave; that the grin upon the living face is not very different from the grin within the skull. But with it there goes the consciousness that there is in life something very strong and enduring, something which has a dignity of its own, however much its expression may on the surface seem a mockery. Life goes on, whatever happens to the individual, and whatever the individual may be.

Take Grandfer Cantle when we first meet him shaking his old bones in something like a *danse macabre* around the beacon on Rainbarrow:

> With his stick in his hand he began to jig a private minuet, a bunch of copper seals shining and swinging like a pendulum from under his waistcoat: he also began to sing, in the voice of a bee up a flue

> The king called down his nobles all,
> By one, by two, by three;

> Earl Mar—shall, I'll go shrive the queen,
> And thou shalt wend with me.

'Want of breath prevented a continuance of the song' after one more verse, and a stander-by, restraining his mirth, comes out with:

> 'A fair stave, Grandfer Cantle; but I'm afeard 'tis too much for the mouldy weasand of such an old man as you,' he said to the wrinkled reveller. 'Dostn't wish th' wast three sixes again, Grandfer, as you was when you first learnt to sing it?'
> 'Hey?' said Grandfer Cantle, stopping in his dance.
> 'Dostn't wish wast young again, I say? There's a hole in thy poor bellows nowadays seemingly.'
> 'But there's good art in me? If I couldn't make a little wind go a long ways I should seem no younger than the most aged man, should I, Timothy?'
> 'And how about the new-married folk down there at the Quiet Woman Inn?' the other inquired. . . . 'What's the rights of the matter about 'em? You ought to know, being an understanding man.'

'But a little rakish, hey? I own to it. Master Cantle is that, or he's nothing. Yet 'tis a gay fault, neighbour Fairway, that age will cure.'

He proposes all should troop off and wish them joy, himself leading them, for it would be very unlike him not to be the first in every spree that 's going. There is something portentous in Grandfer Cantle; he symbolizes the profound Pan-like element which exists, and one may hope, always will exist, in human nature. And to give the sense of ordinary life going on whatever heroes may die, take the little scene after the death of Nelson in *The Dynasts*. That work is undoubtedly his masterpiece, over which he had brooded for many years, making sketches for it, as it were, in *The Trumpet Major*, *Wessex Tales*, and other places. It is his least attackable work, for on that vast scale the wills of men can seem little in comparison with the Immanent Will, without offence to human pride. The scene is at 'Budmouth', in an inn, with boatmen and burghers sitting on settles around the fire, smoking and drinking.

First Burgher. So they've brought him home at last, hey? And he's to be solemnized with a roaring funeral?

First Boatman. Yes, thank God. . . . 'Tis better to lie dry than wet, if can'st do it without stinking on the road gravewards. And they took care that he shouldn't.

Second Boatman. 'Tis to be at Paul's; so they say that know. And the crew of the 'Victory' have to walk in front, and Captain Hardy is to carry his stars and garters on a great velvet pin-cushion. . . .

Second Burgher. And how did they bring him home so that he could lie in state afterwards to the naked eye!

First Boatmen. Well, as they always do,—in a cask of sperrits.

Second Burgher. Really, now!

First Boatman. (lowering his voice) But what happened was this. They were a long time coming, owing to the contrary winds, and the 'Victory' being little more than a wreck. And grog ran short, because they'd used near all they had to peckle his body in. So—they broached the Adm'l.

Second Burgher. How?

First Boatman. Well, the plain calendar of it is, that when he come
to be unhooped, it was found that the crew had drunk him dry.
What was the men to do? Broke down by the battle, and
hardly able to keep afloat, 'twas a most defendable thing, and it
fairly saved their lives. So he was their salvation after death as
he had been in the fight. If he could have knowed, 'twould
have pleased him down to the ground! How 'a would have
laughed through the spigot-hole: 'Draw on, my hearties!
Better I shrivel than you famish.' Ha-ha!
Second Burgher. It may be defendable afloat; but it seems queer
ashore.
First Boatman. Well, that's how I had it from one that knows. . . .
However, let's touch a livelier string. Peter Green, strike up
that new ballet that they've lately had prented here, and were
hawking about town last market-day.
Second Boatman. With all my heart. Though my windypipe's a bit
clogged since the war have made beer so mortal small.

With Hardy it is the broad flow of life that matters, not the
occasional upjetting fountain.

And finally, once more to challenge Mr. Forster, I do
not feel with him that Hardy's novels are 'to give out the
sound of hammer strokes as they proceed'. They are
rather like solemn panoramas gradually unrolled before us.
I do not merely mean that we are in this way conscious of
the lapse of time, though in most novels, in *Tom Jones*, say,
or *Pride and Prejudice*, or *Vanity Fair*, we seem ourselves to
have traversed time, rather than to have seen something
unfold. We get, I think, a little of the same sense of
panorama in *War and Peace*, in *Madame Bovary*, or in that
much more concentrated book, *Wuthering Heights*. What
I mean in contradistinction with resounding hammer
strokes is a quality of silence, the silence of tragedy
brooding over an accidented landscape. The landscape is
inevitable enough, but the figures have a certain limited
freedom, the freedom that we have in life between birth
and death, the movements of joy and suffering, of work and
sympathy and love. What is peculiar is the rhythm of their

movements, something repeated and eternal, like the flux
and reflux of waves upon a beach.   And here, since with
novelists who are also poets it is often easier to cite their
essence from their verse rather than from their prose, let
me quote one of the poems of *War and Patriotism* (not, one
may point out, at all the same thing) called, 'In the Time
of the "Breaking of Nations" '.

I

Only a man harrowing clods
   In a slow silent walk
With an old horse that stumbles and nods
   Half asleep as they stalk.

II

Only thin smoke without flame
   From the heaps of couch-grass;
Yet this will go onward the same
   Though Dynasties pass.

III

Yonder a maid and her wight
   Come whispering by;
Wars' annals will cloud into night
   Ere their story die.

'Only a man harrowing clods'; that is the human movement that seems visible in the Hardy panorama, a movement which keeps a man bowed down over the earth, his
mother, his master, and his slave; that keeps him bowed
down whatever may be the flame of life shining in his eyes,
or the ambitious passions and desires, noble or ignoble,
that guide and animate his heart.   And it will, I think, be
conceded that the movement within the landscape is not
without its dignity.

RUDYARD KIPLING

I

M^R. KIPLING has so scrupulously winnowed the elements of his art, that his candour has deceived many into thinking him too nearly a simpleton to yield much that can be of use to them in exploring life. They are inclined to take too literally Mr. Max Beerbohm's vision of him dancing a jig with Britannia upon Hampstead Heath (after swapping hats with her), and have thought her as much belittled by his bowler as he is made ridiculous by her helmet. But it is really only the high finish of his art which makes him seem to lack subtlety, for he does not display the workings of his mind, his doubts, his gropings. He drives his thought to a conclusion; and it is only when it has reached to force of an intuition, of an assent in Newman's meaning of the word, that he clothes it in appropriate symbols.

He is, one may perhaps claim, romantic by impulse; but then he tries his romance seven times in the fire of actuality, and brings it to the clearness of crystal. Romance, for him, does not lie in yearning, but in fruition: it is not a vague beacon floating in a distant void. It may be

> A veil to draw 'twixt God his Law
> And Man's infirmity,

but that particular throwing up of the sponge, that sort of beglamouring of facts, is not permanently to his taste.

What is more to the credit of romance, in his view, is that, by imagination and faith, it brings up the 9.15. Yet if that were the end, romance itself would be a trivial thing to make such a pother about, even if bringing up the 9.15 does stand for building cities and conquering continents. For even these things are not, in themselves, of vast worth to Mr. Kipling: they are of value only in so far as they are the mechanism which brings action into play. For in the scheme of things as he sees it, action is of the first and final importance, since it is action alone which can make real for man that 'reality', as we say, which is, perhaps, no more than a dream in the mind of Brahma. So small a matter as

> . . . the every day affair of business, meals and clothing
> Builds a Bulkhead 'twixt Despair and the Edge of Nothing,

for man is playing a Great Game of 'To Be, or Not to Be' in the face of an indifferent universe, a universe as indifferent as Hardy's. So man must work, since 'For the pain of the soul there is, outside God's Grace, but one drug; and that is a man's craft, learning, or other helpful motion of his own mind'; and by the last Mr. Kipling means action, since thought by itself is incomplete, and is only made whole through doing.

It is in the story 'The Children of the Zodiac' that Mr. Kipling seems most wholly to express his view; and there we read, 'You cannot pull a plough,' said the bull, with a little touch of contempt, 'I can, and that prevents me thinking of the Scorpion,' namely death. But that is not action as a form of running away from thought, but rather identifying oneself with the material of thought. There is a touch of the tragic about Mr. Kipling. But even so the problem is not so clear and shallow that it can be solved easily, for disillusion lurks even behind useful action, and the void may still be there:

As Adam was a-working outside of Eden-Wall,
He used the Earth, he used the Seas, he used the Air and all;
　And out of black disaster
　He arose to be the master
　　Of Earth and Water, Air and Fire,
　　But never reached his heart's desire!
　　　(The Apple Tree's cut down!)

This disillusion also, it is plain, must be warded off, other-wise work (which is salvation) will not take place; and the Children of the Zodiac did not succeed in warding it off until they had learnt to laugh. Therefore Mr. Kipling also laughs, sometimes to ease his bitterness in this way, but oftener to do more than this; he laughs, not the Bergsonian laughter of social adjustment, but the impas-sioned, defiant laughter of Nietzsche; not the rectifying laughter of comedy, but the healing laughter of farce. Whence 'Brugglesmith', 'The Village that Voted the Earth was Flat', and the immortal, the Puck-like Pyecroft. Man must laugh lest he perish, just as he must work if he is to exist at all.

Yet it must not be thought that by work Mr. Kipling means fuss and hurry; he will have nothing to do with 'indecent restlessness'. As to the battle of life, that good old comforter, he remarks that 'The God who sees us all die knows that there is far too much of that battle', and the man who created Kim's lovable lama is not blind to the possibility that his own means of defeating emptiness and evading the fear of death may be vanity. There is a rift somewhere, and Ganesh in 'The Bridge-Builders' may after all be right in regarding the toil of men but as 'dirt digging in the dirt'. There is, indeed, another possibility, and the problem is neatly put in the *Bhagavadgītā*, where Arjuna says: 'Oh Krishna, thou speakest in paradoxes, for first thou dost praise renunciation, and then praisest thou the performance of service through actions. Pray which of them has the greater merit?' It is only after some hesitation that Krishna answers, 'Verily, I say unto thee, that of the two, the performance of service is preferable to the renunciation of action.'

But there must be something behind action to justify it, and with Mr. Kipling it is a love of loyalty which reinforces his philosophy of action. First of all there is that of man to man, a loyalty born of understanding of a man's work, and the wholeness of his character. But personal loyalty, if infinitely valuable, is also horribly rare, and Mr. Kipling has no exaggerated faith in it; he has come not to hope overmuch of man. 'The raw fact of life,' Pharaoh Akhenaton told him, 'is that mankind is just a little lower than the angels, and the conventions are based on that fact in order that men may become angels. But if you begin by the convention that men are angels, they will assuredly become bigger beasts than ever.' And loyalty is an angelic quality.

This takes us a long way from the 'personal relation', which, as we shall see, figures so large in recent literature; and, indeed, what distinguishes Mr. Kipling from so many present-day writers is precisely that he does not attempt to break down man's loneliness, seeing only futility in the balm of the 'personal relation'.

> Chase not with undesired largesse
>   Of sympathy the heart
> Which, knowing her own bitterness
>   Presumes to dwell apart.

That is why, when Mulvaney told him the story of 'The Courting of Dinah Shadd', the catastrophic tale of his wooing, Mr. Kipling said nothing; he gave him a hand, which can help, but cannot heal: for at the moment when a man's black hour descends upon him, he has to fight it out alone. 'When I woke I saw Mulvaney, the night dewgemming his moustache, leaning on his rifle at picket, lonely as Prometheus on his rock, with I know not what vultures tearing his liver.'

But since man is thus unavoidably lonely among men, there is another loyalty to serve as a spring of action, and that is a devotion to something each man must conceive of as bigger than himself.   Power man has, yet

> It is not given
> For goods or gear,
> But for the Thing,

whatever the Thing may be.   Mr. Kipling does not even admit the last infirmity of noble mind, for fame does not count.   Thus more than sympathy, admiration, and love, go out from him to obscure men with whom 'heroism, failure, doubt, despair, and self-abnegation' are daily matters, and about whom the official reports are silent. His heart is given at once to any person who strives to do a thing well, not for praise, but through sheer love of the craftsman.   For him, as for Parolles, self-love is 'the most inhibited sin in the canon'; and, after all, 'one must always risk one's life or one's soul, or one's peace—or some little thing.'

Here then, we see the scale of Mr. Kipling's values. First it is essential to accept the world for what it is with no romantic illusions, to play the man while the odds are eternally and crushingly against you.   It is hopeless to try to alter the world.   Even if you are capable of adding to it, if yours is not the appointed time your work will be sacrificed, as the medieval priest in *Debits and Credits* had to smash his microscope, and the Elizabethan seaman in *Rewards and Fairies* had to abandon his idea of iron ships: the time was not yet.   But man must not complain, nor ask for life's handicap to be reduced.   ' "My right!" Ortheris answered with deep scorn.   "My right! I ain't a recruity to go whining about my rights to this and my rights to that, just as if I couldn't look after myself. My rights! 'Strewth A'mighty! I'm a man''.' It is that kind of individuality, that kind of integrity, proud and secure in its own fortress, which constitutes the aristocracy which alone is worth while, which alone can play the Great Game of actuality.

An aristocrat is, for Mr. Kipling, one who, whatever his race or caste or creed, has a full man within him: Ortheris, Tallantire of the frontier district, Mahbub Ali, M'Andrew, a whole host of them, all are aristocrats, as is Hobden the labourer, with his sardonic smile at the changes of landlords and the unchangeableness of things. They are aristocrats because they care little for themselves in comparison with what they stand for, because they are generous, and play the Great Game with laughter on their lips, seeking nobody's help, and claiming no reward. 'First a man must suffer, then he must learn his work, and the self-respect that that knowledge brings.' Never mind if he is a failure, a tramp, or a drunkard, he may yet be an aristocrat, if he keeps himself whole, and does not set an undue value upon his feelings. This band of chosen naturally hates the intriguers of Simla, or the Tomlinsons, who, when they die in their houses in Berkeley Square, deserve neither heaven nor hell. It despises the self-styled 'intellectuals' who 'deal with people's insides from the point of view of men who have no stomachs'. It loathes the rabble which whimpers, and the elements which ruin the industrious hive, crying to the workers, 'Come here, you dear downy duck, and tell us about your feelings.' The mob which denies the loneliness of man is hateful to it, for the mob has accomplished nothing, and always defiles what it cannot understand. Thus Mr. Kipling's Utopia, unlike Mr. Wells's, is one where privacy must not be violated, and where men slink away when they find themselves part of a crowd, loathing the claims of 'the People', who can be crueller than kings. Moreover, Mr. Kipling has only contempt for those who would marshal and pigeon-hole mankind, making it nicely tidy and neat; he feels they are ignorant of men, shallow in their analysis of motives, 'since the real reasons which make or break a man are too absurd or too obscene to be reached from the outside.' And it follows that for him 'social reform' is the selfish game of the idle.

With this aristocratic preference there goes, as so often, a sense of some Divine Ruler, for to whom else is man to dedicate his work? But Mr. Kipling has no especial choice in this direction, is no sectarian, thinking that 'when a man has come to the turnstiles of Night, all the creeds in the world seem to him wonderfully alike and colourless'. He asks of a creed only that it shall give a man the virtues he admires. 'I tell you now that the faith that takes care that every man shall keep faith, even though he may save his soul by breaking faith, is the faith for a man to believe in.' He has small opinion of Christianity because it has not eliminated the fear of the end, so that the Western world 'clings to the dread of death more closely than to the hope of life'. However, he is very tender to other people's beliefs, for men, after all, need a respite. Thus he writes of a Burmese temple, that 'Those that faced the figures prayed more zealously than the others, so I judged that their troubles were the greater'. For when all has been written and acted, his own faith also may be subject to disillusion; so with perfect consistency he may urge us 'be gentle while the heathen pray to Buddha at Kamakura'.

This, oddly enough, brings us back to Hampstead Heath, for once we speak of Mr. Kipling's religion, we speak of the British Empire. Mr. Beerbohm was cruel in his caricature, but also wittier than he appears at first sight, for he made Mr. Kipling look a little unhappy at having thus blatantly to parade the lady of his homage. Yet one must agree that Mr. Kipling cannot be dissociated from the British Empire. It would almost seem that his mission was to bind it together in one blood-brotherhood, a purposive Masonic lodge, whose business it is to cleanse the world of shoddy. Nor can he altogether escape the suspicion of having been dazzled by it. He is enraptured by the vision of men clean of mind and thew, clear of eye and inward sight, spreading over the earth, their lands bound by the ships which fly over the sea like shuttles, weaving the clan together. His is no mere politician's picture of red on the map, since Britannia for him is a goddess. She is a goddess not only by the fact of her being, but in her nature, for she exacts much toil from her votaries, much of the silent endurance, abnegation, and loyalty that he loves. The Empire then is to be cherished, not so much because it is in itself an achievement, but because, like old Rome, it is the most superb instrument to cause men to outface the universe, assert himself against vacancy. Since it unifies the impulses needed to do this, it is Mr. Kipling's Catholic Church.

These things being, apparently, the basis of Mr. Kipling's thought (though the Empire is, strictly speaking, only an accident, an expression rather than a necessity), we may now ask ourselves, honestly facing the risk of being impudent and unduly probing, of what impulses this thought is the satisfaction. And at the foundation of his philosophic love of action we are tempted to find that pining for action men often have, when, for one reason or another, it is denied them. He sometimes comes near to blaspheming against his art, echoing James Thomson's

> Singing is sweet, but be sure of this;
> Lips only sing when they cannot kiss,

as though the mere act of writing were itself proof of impotence or frustration. This is not a final attitude, but it indicates what may lie behind Mr. Kipling's adoration of perfectly insufferable and not altogether real subalterns, and others, who in various degrees (so long as it is not from offices) handle the affairs of the world.

Yet, ultimately, he is too good a craftsman, too whole an artist, not to see that God, or whatever other name he may be known by, is to be praised in more ways than the obvious. Nevertheless, he now and again reaches out for support to the knowledge that he also is playing the great game, if not of the universe, at least of the world, and is as worthy of a number as Kim, Mahbub Ali, or Hurree Babu:

> Who once hath dealt in the widest game
>   That all of a man can play,
> No later love, no larger fame
>   Will lure him long away.
> As the war-horse smelleth the battle afar,
>   The entered Soul, no, less
> He saith 'Ha! Ha!' where the trumpets are
>   And the thunders of the Press.

Such an attitude permanently held would be far too jejune to produce the real intensity of vision we get from Mr. Kipling; and luckily for us, he has at bottom that worship of his own craft he so much admires in others. Addressing his God, his subtilized Jehovah, who judges man by his deeds, he says:

> Who lest all thought of Eden fade
>   Bring'st Eden to the craftsman's brain,
> God-like to muse on his own trade,
>   And Man-like stand with God again.

There he is the priest of the Mysterious Will, who causes all things to come in their due time; but one feels he still sometimes needs to justify his work to himself. He is urged to make it plain that all his stories are parables. Thus:

> When all the world would have a matter hid,
> Since truth is seldom friend to any crowd,
> Men write in fable, as old Æsop did,
> Jesting at that which none will name aloud.
> And this they needs must do, or it will fall
> Unless they please, they are not heard at all.

It is clear that for Mr. Kipling, art is not an escape: it is a precision of bare facts, which his art must make palatable.

Further, since the choice of a goddess does not lie altogether within a man's mental scope, we may seek in Mr. Kipling's impulses the reason for his profound satisfaction in the Empire, and his need to assert it. Perhaps the most important of these is his craving to belong to something, a love, not of 'the little platoon', to use Burke's phrase, but of the large regiment. 'It must be pleasant to have a country of one's own to show off,' he remarks. Indeed, his craving for roots makes even the deck of a P. and O. British soil; British, not English, because he is a citizen of the Empire, not of England alone: for if it were essential to be the latter, he would be partly dispossessed. Having spent so many of his early years in India, he is not wholly of England: indeed, India is the place where he really belongs. When, for instance, in 1913, he visited Cairo, he wrote: 'It is true that the call to prayer, the cadence of some of the street cries, and the cut of some of the garments differed a little from what I had been brought up to; but for the rest, the shadow on the dial had turned back twenty degrees for me, and I found myself saying, as perhaps the dead say when they have recovered their wits, "This is my real world again!" ' But he is not an Indian, he is an Englishman; therefore, to be an integral whole, he must at all costs make England and the Empire one.

His love of the Empire, and his admiration for those virtues it brings out in men, make him apt to find qualities in Englishmen only which really exist in all races; and this is part of the deformation Mr. Kipling the artist has at times undergone at the hands of Mr. Kipling the man of action, who found his weapon in the press, and his altar in the Empire. If there had been no daily, or weekly, or monthly papers, he might have remained a priest; but in his middle days he fell into the encouraging hands of W. E. Henley, then, in 1893, editing *The National Observer*. Though this gave his talent scope, it meant that instead of speaking only to those who would understand his very special philosophy, he began to proselytize, and shout too loud into the deaf ears of Demos. His work suffered by the accidents of time and circumstance, by the mischance that he was born into an age of magazines and newspapers, when the listeners are the many, and not the aristocrats to whom he naturally belongs. It took him, with his slightly unhappy expression, on to Hampstead Heath. A change came over his work, and the echo of the voice of Henley 'throwing a chest' (another man of action to whom action was denied) is every now and again heard between the lines. In 1893 he published *Many Inventions*, a rich, varied, and mature work which might be singled out as the best volume of his stories, unless *Life's Handicap* be preferred; but from that year, when he joined Henley, his writing took on a more obviously didactic hue, and we have *The Day's Work*, such parables as 'A Walking Delegate', that tale of perfectly dutiful horses kicking the Trades-Union-Agitator horse. In 1887, or thereabouts, he was writing his delightful *Letters of Marque*, with their profound tolerance of India: in 1907 he wrote for *The Morning Post* the clangorous *Letters to the Family*. The man who had in earlier years remarked 'He began to understand why Boondi does not encourage Englishmen', could later complain 'Yet South Africa could even now be made a tourists' place—if only the railroad and the steamship lines had faith'. That is shocking. It is true that he had always loved the Empire, but not in the Hampstead Heath way; and surely it was the exigencies of this later didactic journalism which turned him from a priest into an advance booking agent, and forced him into too extravagant a statement of 'British' qualities. He does not, however, in all his work assume that these are the monopoly of the British, for he awards his due to the Frenchman and the Sikh, and even to the Bengali, when he really gives rein to his profound instincts, and forgets the thunders of the press. Therefore the distortion does not matter in the long run, for time and again he gives us things of a breadth and a peculiar grip we get from no other writer of his generation.

The accidents, then, of Mr. Kipling's attitude may be dismissed, to allow us to return to his intuitions, and proceed to the next step in our analysis, namely, a consideration of what symbols he has chosen to clothe his intuitions in. He has usually chosen men and women to body forth his notions—his plots have no great symbolic importance; and thus his people, as is always the case in really creative art, represent something beyond themselves. They are not merely vehicles for an idle tale. Where he has chosen other material, as in 'The Mother Hive', or 'The Ship that Found Herself', he has failed, as any one is bound to do. An apologue always smacks of the schoolroom, and it is worth noticing that these stories belong to his most didactic period. He is not quite at his ease there, his assent is a little forced; but when his intuition was whole, as in *Kim*, in which the artist conquers the moralist and buries him deep under ground, he is nothing short of superb: his symbols clothe his intuition so that we take it for flesh and blood. That is, we work from life to the thought, and not from the thought to life, as we do with lesser artists, who have ideas they wish to impose upon life. Mr. Kipling's failures occur either when his shallower, demagogue nature takes charge, and we are conscious of didacticism; or where the intuition is uncompleted. It is uncompleted in two sets of instances: the first where women are concerned, whence Mrs. Hauksbee, Mrs. Gadsby, and others, where the symbols are vulgar because the intuition is false (there is a reservation to be made in the case of the woman in the last story in *Debits and Credits*); the second is in the mysterious world of unreality which he feels about him, but which he has not resolved within himself: hence such failures—one must here defy popular opinion—as 'They', and 'The Brushwood Boy'. There the symbols are sentimental, not because the intuition is feeble, but because it has not been resolved into art.

So far an attempt has been made to define Mr. Kipling's philosophic apparatus; but without delight, and perhaps an attitude of praise, there can be no great art after his manner, and these he has abundantly. *A Diversity of Creatures*; that is not only the title of a book, it is a phrase which occurs often in other of his volumes, and he often thanks God for the variety of His beings. He is an apt illustration for those who claim that only by adoring what is can one add to life; and *quia multum amavit* is a passport to his heaven. He revels in men so long as they are positive, since it is only by his deeds that man can exist. Also, with a generous sensuality which rejects no physical sensation, he loves 'the good brown earth', especially the smells that it produces, West or East. With all these likes, with his keen senses, his recognition of adventure in life and his feeling for romance in works, and his zestful following of men on their occasions lawful and unlawful, he has God's plenty within him.

Thus it is that his best symbols also have God's plenty within them. It is noticeable that they are not like those of Tchekov, say, or of Henry James, since different symbols correspond with different intuitions, and his are not theirs. There is nothing rarefied about them. Mr. Kipling's live close to the ground, and he has frequented the more primitive sort of men because 'all the earth is full of tales to him who listens and does not drive the poor away from his door. The poor are the best of tale-tellers, for they must lay their ear to the ground every night.' He met a hundred men on the road to Delhi, and they were all his brothers, since they lived close to the actualities that can be handled. They were the people in *Kim*, there were Peachey Carnehan and Daniel Dravot (in 'The Man Who Would be King'); there were forgotten toilers in out-stations, and above all there were Mulvaney, Ortheris, and Learoyd. Nor must it pass unnoticed that all his three soldiers had trodden paths of bitterness ('first a man must suffer'), and were at times subject to an overwhelming sorrow akin to madness, the sorrow of disillusion. They are of value as symbols precisely because they have outfaced much. They were none of them obviously successful, for Mr. Kipling despises success except that which consists in keeping one's soul intact. Whence his sympathy for those who are broken because they are too positive, such as the sometime Fellow of an Oxford college who had passed 'outside the pale', for the lighthouse man who went mad because of the infernal streakiness of the tides, and even for Love o' Women. In such cases, where human beings seem wholly to live the life of the symbol and to exist as a quality, Mr. Kipling is content that men should be no more than a part of the earth; he is happy to be their interpreter, and give them their place as players of the Great Game.

If, at this point, we try to mark what it is that most distinguishes Mr. Kipling from other writers of our period, we find that he shares with most the despondency of the day, but not its optimism as regards panaceas such as support Mr. Wells and Mr. Shaw; and that his delight in the actuality of men, in their proven virtues, gives him values instead of vague hopes. In his metaphysical scepticism, in his belief in the void which surrounds existence he is a child of his time, as modern as any of our literary nihilists who see, in Mr. Houseman's phrase, that 'when men think they fasten their hands upon their hearts'. Indeed, it is safe to say that at no modern period has the world seemed so empty a thing, the universe so indifferent, our values so factitious; and as we look back upon the centuries we can see that this attitude has been fatefully coming upon us. Yet, though Mr. Kipling manifests this attitude, he differs from his contemporaries, and it is because of this difference that he already seems to survive them. He is more enduring, because something of the past three centuries clings to him.

For the Elizabethans and Jacobeans, life gained its glamour largely from its nearness to the plague-pit; its values were determined and heightened by the vigorously expressed dogmas of a church which, for pulpit reasons at least, believed in Hell; the metaphysical void was filled with a sense that life was given man as a discipline and an adventure: this is still part of Mr. Kipling's belief. Indeed, if one were to have to choose one man from whom he descends rather than another, one would light upon Jeremy Taylor. In *Holy Dying* we read:

> Softness is for slaves and beasts, for minstrels and useless persons, for such as cannot ascend higher than the state of a fair ox, or a servant entertained for vainer offices: but the man that designs his son for noble employments, to honours and to triumphs, to consular dignities and presidencies of councils, loves to see him pale with study, or panting with labour, hardened with sufferance, or eminent by dangers. And so God dresses us for heaven.

And in *Letters of Travel* Mr. Kipling writes:

> I wonder sometimes whether any eminent novelist, philosopher,

dramatist, or divine of to-day, has to exercise half the pure imagination, not to mention insight, endurance, and self-restraint, which is
accepted without comment in what is called 'the material exploita-
tion' of a new country.   Take only the question of creating a new
city at the juncture of two lines—all three in the air.   The mere
drama of it, the play of human virtues, would fill a book.   And when
the work is finished, when the city is, when the new lines embrace
a new belt of farms, and the tide of wheat has rolled North another
unexpected degree, the men who did it break off, without compli-
ments, to repeat the joke elsewhere.

The mind is the same; the matter only the difference of
the centuries.

Then, with the advance of science and the retreat of the
plague, man grew less concerned with himself and heaven,
and more interested in the outer world, its marvels, its
emerging order.   Coupled with a somewhat flabby Deism,
believing at the most in only a luke-warm Hell, was the
attitude of mind typified by John Evelyn, who, like Mr.
Kipling, found naught common on the earth.   Here Mr.
Kipling largely stays, and with the introspective movement
which found its prophet in Rousseau, with the hysterical
subjective idealists whose only reality is their emotion, he
will have nothing to do, and it is likely that Proust seems
a dreary waste to him.   He cannot away with men and
women intent upon saving their souls, or who believe even,
that they have souls worth the saving.   It is typical that he
should describe a man he dislikes as 'fearing physical pain
as some men fear sin'.

Yet the solipsist attitude still further weakened the idea
of future punishment, and we are not surprised that in the
century and a half which saw its development, an English
Lord Chancellor, Lord Westbury, should, in a famous
judgement, have 'dismissed Hell with costs, and taken away
from orthodox members of the Church of England their
last hope of everlasting damnation'.   This was to have its
effect; but habits of impulse are slow to change, and if

there was to be no Hell, there was still to be service to God; and of this sense again Mr. Kipling retains something, since, as far as meaning goes, it might have been not he, but Browning who wrote:

> One instant's toil to Thee denied
> Stands all eternity's offence.

But soon it came to be seen that if there was no Hell, the only Heaven would have to be on earth; and if social reform began at least as early as Shaftesbury, not to go back to Shelburne, it is chiefly characteristic of the Edwardian period.   Mr. Kipling, however, who cannot bear the flaccidity of social reform, its interference of people with each other, still has a hope of Hell; and agreeing that this world suffices for man, places his Hell upon earth.   Thus he cannot accept our modern Utopias, so neat and hygienic, so free from temptation and sin and suffering—except, for him, the suffering of being in a crowd.   Utopian perfection would be loathsomely insipid, and we may surmise that the final reason why the British Empire satisfies him, is that it can contain both Heaven and Hell, at least as much as is good for any man.

Apart from the delight which he gives, an important reservation, it is doubtful if the real value of any writer is apparent to his close contemporaries: his equals in age are likely to seize upon those things they already share with him, rather than greet what is original; and, with mankind's aversion for what is new in ideas, reject what the next generation will eagerly clutch at.   As far as can be judged at present, the elements in Mr. Kipling's work which have won him popularity are the least important, the most ephemeral.   It will only be possible to give him his rightful place when the political heats of his day have become coldly historical.   But to us, the successive generation, he has a value that may well be permanent, apart from his language, which itself deserves to live. He has indicated an attitude towards life which, to us groping for a solid basis, may serve, if not for that basis itself, then as a point of disagreement. He deals, after all, with the enduring problems of humanity, the problems out of which all religion, all real poetry must arise. Moreover, he provides a solution which those of his own cast of mind— and they are many, though most may be unaware of it— will greet with satisfaction, and even with that sense of glamour, of invigoration, which it is partly the function of good literature to give.

II

THE BREAKING STRAIN, HEALING AND COMPASSION

THE more one reads Kipling, the more complex and baffling he becomes: and here I would like to bring forward a highly individual, recurring, and important element in his make-up which has hardly been noticed. It is, perhaps, very relevant to our present-day atmosphere of strain, our *angst* if you like to call it so. A great deal has been written about him in the last twenty years, not only here but in France, Italy, and latterly in America, mainly about his prose; but since this aspect has been missed, something always nags at my mind telling me: ' No; that isn't quite what he meant. It isn't there exactly that he matters.'

Something more, it is true, has been done about his poetry, notably by Mr. T. S. Eliot in his enormously valuable study; but what he actually chose for his anthology is, if only by accident, a trifle tendentious, because he was making out the case for Kipling as a superb ballad and hymn writer. He was far more than that, far subtler and more sensitive, as hinted, but not much more than hinted, by Mr. T. R. Henn in *The Apple and the Spectroscope*. Many of the poems, moreover, are complementary to the stories, poem and story making a complete whole. But, taken all in all, in nearly everything written about him the discussion is still too much overshadowed by politics (the process of shedding this aspect is taking longer than I hoped earlier), as, for example, in Mr. Edmund Wilson's *The Wound and the Bow*. Surely now that the tumult and the shouting have died, it ought to be possible to see Kipling objectively: he is no longer part of the political picture.

It is not to be denied that one has to look at his imperialism. But it was not chauvinistic, as most people used to think—and some still do—since he always up-braided the jingo. Actually, his conception of the Empire was in the tradition of the great myth of beneficent world-government which stirred Shakespeare when he wrote the final speech of Cranmer in *Henry VIII*, which comes out in D'avenant, and still more grandly in Dryden's *Annus Mirabilis* and Pope's *Windsor Forest*. It was a poetic idea. Further, the Empire was important for Kipling, because, as explained in my earlier essay, it was something a man could devote himself to, an object of the kind of faith Kipling was always looking for. Having seen men broken, in soul as well as in body, through selflessly carrying out the daily work of the Empire, unthanked, unrewarded, even reviled, he gave the Empire his *conditional* allegiance.

And then, because he accepted, especially in his early days, the fact that men did horrible things to each other, he could not be a philosophic 'optimist', à *la* Shaftesbury, but was, rather, a 'pessimist' in the line of Swift. He could not help, therefore, rejecting the idea of man as a benevolent creature, and in so doing he trod on a good many 'advanced' toes. As a result he is continually being accused of illiberalism, as, for instance, by Professor Lionel Trilling in his fine book *The Liberal Imagination*. How far Kipling may have been right in that respect, as against his critics, the history of the world in the last fifty years may help us to judge.

It is not, however, the purpose here to defend Kipling on that sort of issue; it is, rather, to penetrate a region which nobody seems to have explored,[1] into something which more than offsets that apparently callous, almost cruel element in him which outrages a good many people, and made Harold Laski say that Kipling 'will symbolize the literature of hate, of malignant grandiosity'. This attitude persists; we get, for instance, Professor V. de S. Pinto in his *Crisis in English Poetry* regarding him as the apostle of brute force. Nothing can be further from the truth. He symbolizes not hate, but a deep compassion; not malignant grandiosity and brute force, but humility, and tenderness amounting to deep pity. Re-reading him, especially his later work, one cannot but be impressed by this note of his, repeatedly and emphatically struck; and, more significant still, by his intense interest about, one might say his deep feeling for, healing, and the means of healing.

First, however, must be noted a curious thread which runs through all his work, which can be described only as his 'descents into hell', not only into those places where the soul is lonely and has to face itself, but into the over-whelming hells that blot out. Take this description:

. . . Just then . . . I was aware of a little grey shadow, as it might have been a snowflake seen against the light, floating at an immense distance in the background of my brain. It annoyed me, and I shook my head to get rid of it. Then my brain telegraphed that it was the fore-runner of a swift-striding gloom. . . . The gloom overtook me . . . and my amazed and angry soul dropped, gulf by gulf, into that horror of great darkness which is spoken of in the Bible.

[1] This was written before the appearance of the admirable *The Art of Rudyard Kipling*, by J. M. S. Tompkins.

That passage, outrageously cut, is from 'The House Surgeon', a story in *Actions and Reactions*, and it is followed by a poem, which, if pondered, is horrifying, but which some have found insensitive, perhaps because it is written in the direct language and simple rhythm of hymns:

> If thought can reach to Heaven
> On Heaven let it dwell,
> For fear that Thought be given
> Like power to reach to Hell.

—lines which are revealing enough. Similarly, a typical periodical descent into the abyss overtakes the two people of the story 'In the Same Boat', to be found in *A Diversity of Creatures*, as early as 1917. And in his last two books Kipling again and again returns to the theme of the great darkness.

He had touched on the same sort of thing in his earlier stories. There is, for instance, 'At the End of the Passage' in *Life's Handicap*, which came out in 1891, in which the desperately overworked Indian civilian dies because, as his servant commented, he had descended into the Dark Places. From the beginning, then, Kipling had been drawn to tales of mental breakdown, of suffering made unbearable from one cause or another: that, say, of the lighthouse keeper who went mad from loneliness, or the reproved subaltern who shot himself in despair. There are dozens of them. But a change came over his treatment of the theme. In his younger days he was eager only to tell the stories as part of the enthralling, darkly striated pageant of life; later he became interested in the causes, and finally he was absorbed in the healing of the horror, the point to be expanded here. Obviously he knew all about the horror; as he said after the extract quoted, the state 'has to be experienced to be appreciated', and you do not have to read far to know how agonisingly he had himself

experienced it.   Perhaps that is why to some people he
seems so callous about physical pain; he certainly despised
people who feared it, knowing that it was nothing com-
pared with spiritual agony.   This he stated unequivocally
in the 'Hymn to Physical Pain', of which the first and last
stanzas run:

> Dread Mother of Forgetfulness
>   Who, when Thy reign begins,
> Wipest away the Soul's distress,
>   And memory of her sins. . . .
>
> Wherefore we praise Thee in the deep,
>   And on our beds we pray
> For Thy return that Thou may'st keep
>   The Pains of Hell at bay!

It is clear that Kipling, who suffered a good deal of physical
pain in his later life, was at intervals catastrophically
disturbed.

Looking at the stories concerned with these states, you
see that they all come about from too much strain on
people.   The sense of this probably lay far back in Kipling's
experience, when, as a small boy living in the house at
Southsea while his parents were in India, he underwent the
purgatory he was to describe in the terrible story 'Baa,
Baa, Black Sheep'.   But the early tales which have as their
climax a breakdown from strain do not on the whole take
the matter any further; in the later stories, however,
Kipling became, significantly, interested not so much in the
states of horror themselves, as in their cure; the cure, if
you like, of neuroses which are the effects of strain, usually
caused by devotion to duty (often in the war), but sometimes through the operation of sheer fate.   Together with
this, Kipling grew to be ever more deeply interested in the
amount of strain a human being could stand without
breaking down.   Partly to resolve this, he evolved those

strange stories which pictured what he called 'The Order Above' (which, by a sort of inverted Platonism, he regarded as a reflection of 'The Order Below'), symbolized by the Archangels, Satan, and other heavenly principalities and powers. In the last of these tales, 'Uncovenanted Mercies', the souls of men and women are 'reconditioned' for service as guardian angels, the final point of the process being, as Satan puts it, 'a full test for Ultimate Breaking Strain'. The technical phrase struck Kipling, and the year before his death he published the 'Hymn of Breaking Strain', the load to which men are ruthlessly subjected. A portion of it reads:

> The careful text-books measure
> (Let all who build beware!)
> The load, the shock, the pressure
> Material can bear. . . .
>
> But, in our daily dealing
> With stone and steel, we find
> The Gods have no such feeling
> Of justice toward mankind.
> To no set gauge they make us,—
> For no laid course prepare—
> And presently o'ertake us
> With loads we cannot bear:
> *Too merciless to bear.*

But Kipling will not encourage whining. The poem tells us at the end, that if man serves 'the veiled and secret Power, in spite of being broken, because of being broken', he can stand up and build anew.

If, then, the world includes hells for men and women so intolerable that the strain actually breaks them, what is the cure? Kipling had all sorts of mechanisms for healing, varieties of psycho-analysis which clear up complexes. But these are merely mechanisms, and the driving force, the

virtue without which no cure can be effective, is—and this
can be boldly stated—compassion. He realized very early,
as an intuition, with what Newman would have called
'complete assent', that man is fated to suffer and to be
lonely; that when a man's black hour descends upon him
he has to fight it out alone, indeed would rather fight it out
alone, as did Mulvaney—himself, incidentally, a healer.
When in *Debits and Credits* he said that 'for the pain of the
soul there is, outside God's grace, but one drug . . .'
stress must be placed on God's grace, which is compassion.
One becomes, perhaps startlingly, aware of this from the
story 'The Gardener' in the same volume. This is concerned with a woman whose adored natural son—whom
she passes off as her nephew—is killed in the war. She
goes to the war cemetery to visit his grave, and finds there
a man firming in the young plants, who asks, 'What are you
looking for?' She gives the name and adds: 'My nephew'.
The story ends:

> The man lifted his eyes and looked at her with infinite com-
> passion before he turned from the fresh-sown grass toward the naked
> black crosses.
> 'Come with me,' he said, 'and I will show you where your son
> lies.'
> When Helen left the cemetery she turned for a last look. In the
> distance she saw the man bending over his young plants; and she
> went away, supposing him to be the gardener.

Though Kipling may not have been in any ordinary
sense of the word a Christian, it would seem clear that this
Gospel reference to Mary Magdalene meeting Christ at the
Tomb is profoundly revealing of his attitude. If this were
an isolated case, it would not perhaps count for much:
but the attitude is evident again and again, as in 'Uncovenanted Mercies', already touched upon. After Satan's
remark about the Ultimate Breaking Strain the story goes
on: ' "But now?" Gabriel demanded. "Why do you

ask?'' ''Because it was written *Even Evil itself shall pity*.'' '
It may be noted too that the choruses of the poem which
concludes the similar story 'On the Gate' in *Debits and
Credits* consist, certainly, of Glories, Powers, and Toils,
but also—and this one ought to notice—of Patiences,
Faiths, Hopes, *and Loves*.

This point could be illustrated over and over; but now
attention may be drawn to the remarkable series of stories
which treat of healing, especially those in the later
volumes, 'the Kipling that nobody reads', as G. M. Young
put it in his article in *The Dictionary of National Biography*.
Kipling was perpetually interested in doctors and doctoring, and was much the friend of the famous Sir John Bland
Sutton, who figures as Sir James Belton in the story 'The
Tender Achilles' in Kipling's last collection. Time and
again he demands of medical research less thinking and
more imagination; let us have bolder speculation, he
begged the doctors, rather than improved technique. He
himself had amazing, not to say visionary, notions about
healing. He touched on them first, to any degree, in 'A
Doctor of Medicine'—*Rewards and Fairies*—where the
seventeenth-century astrologer-physician, Nicolas Culpeper, utters very strange doctrine. Kipling dared develop
such notions in an after-dinner speech made to the Royal
Society of Medicine in 1928, when he made a plea for
doctoring to return—on a modern basis—to the astrologi-
cal idea of 'influences'. He argued that: 'Nicolas Culpeper, were he with us now, would find that the essential
unity of creation is admitted in so far forth as we have
plumbed infinity; and that man, Culpeper's epitome of all,
is in himself a universe of universes, each universe ordered
—negatively and positively—by sympathy and antipathy—
on the same lines as hold the stars in their courses.' Soon
he put some of these ideas into the story 'Unprofessional',
where the medical men study what seem to be tides in

malignant tissues. They discuss radium, as astrologers might discuss planetary influences, the analogy Kipling had made use of in his speech to the Royal Society of Medicine. No doubt he knew that all this was the wildest speculation —yet, was it so daft? One of the people in the story says: 'It's crazy mad,' but another retorts, 'Which was what the Admiralty said at first about steam in the Navy.' Some of the tales, as already noted, are on a more psycho-analytical level, and at least two of his cases of war neurosis are cured by what might be called Freudian therapeutics.

Yet healing, that urgent business, might be brought about by other means—even by laughter, which for Kipling, as for Meredith, was always one of the great healers. Another story from his last book, 'The Miracle of St. Jubanus', will serve to illustrate this. The centre of the tale is a village priest, drawn with extraordinary tenderness and understanding. One of his parishioners is a returned peasant-soldier suffering from what we used to call, a little euphemistically, shell-shock. He was one of those who, in the priest's words, 'entered hells of whose existence they had not dreamed—of whose terrors they lacked words to tell'. He would 'hide himself for an hour or two, and come back visibly replunged in his torments'. Being made to laugh restored him from near-idiocy to normality. Kipling, then, sought every way of cure; he was passionately concerned to relieve the sufferings of humanity which, in the last resort, can end only in death. Time and again one finds in him an immense pity, especially for those who, as he liked to put it, had fought with the beasts at Ephesus, beasts far more terrible than the actual beasts of the Epistle of St. Paul. Though not, to repeat, so far as one can judge, a Christian, one could perhaps say that he adhered to the perennial philosophy and verged on mysticism; certainly he shared with the Hindus their tolerance of all attempts to bear the burden of the mystery:

O ye who tread the Narrow Way
By Tophet-flare to Judgment Day,
Be gentle when 'the heathen' pray
To Buddha at Kamakura!

It did not matter to him where a man got his beliefs, so long as his religion could tell him what is said in II. *Samuel* xxv.14: 'Yet God doth devise that his banished be not expelled from him.' Surely those are not the words of a man who symbolizes the literature of hate and malignity, but of one who, for all his rough scorns, and his sometimes infuriating blindness to the other side of the question, symbolizes, rather, a profound, understanding compassion.

E. M. FORSTER

IN choosing novelists of the younger school, I have kept two main needs in view. I thought they should be writers who, while they join up easily with the old traditional line, yet clearly represent the newer generation. And since I believe that tradition is largely a question of form, I have avoided writers who are trying to evolve a new one, such as, easily first, Mrs. Virginia Woolf; and all the more those who, like Mr. James Joyce and Mr. Wyndham Lewis, are, as well as inventing original forms, labouring to re-invent the language. Thus I am not wishing to extract an order of merit from among the half-dozen or so people it appears worth while to consider at all, but to give some reason for my choice. I might, perhaps, have lighted upon Mr. F. M. Ford, but that he does not lend himself readily to analysis, and would demand a deal of quotation.

It may have been noticed that by my first sentence I implied that there is what may be called a new 'school', which is trying to make the novel do something other than the work the older generation asked of it. I suggested thereby that there is no radical difference between a novel by Hardy and one by Thackeray, Scott, or Fielding, but that there is one between those by Mrs. Woolf and, say, those by Mr. Kipling or Mr. George Moore. Some rather younger living writers still clearly belong to the older tradition, Mr. Galsworthy, Mr. Bennett, and indeed most others, what they have in common being an acceptance of life in its social aspects. 'This is what life is like,' they say, and proceed to describe society for us. Mr. Wells, it must be admitted, says, 'Oh no! life's not like that, it's like this—or at any rate it ought to be,' and then goes on to construct Utopias in which mind and body alike are swept clean in a dazzling system of super-sanitation; but that does not really distinguish him from the older school. In fact, he deals more than ever with society.

A question will certainly have asked itself by now. If the new novelists do not say, 'This is what life is like,' what on earth is it they do say? Naturally, it is, in a sense, the business of the artist to show us what he believes life to be like. The business of the novelist, especially, is to let us further into life, to show us a corner of life of which he makes us understand everything, know everything, accept everything. But the new school, on the whole, seems not to make statements so much as to ask questions. It does not say, 'This is what life is like,' but rather, 'Is life really like this?' For the novelist nowadays has an extraordinarily difficult task; he has lost his background, the old established values, the enduring social customs. The framework has gone. Mrs. Woolf solves the problem deliciously by leaving out the background altogether; Mr. Joyce weaves a fantastic background out of human viscera, and one may say in passing, that whatever his *Ulysses* may not be, it is beyond doubt a superb *tour de force*, a triumph of consummate craftsmanship. Mr. Lawrence, as we shall see, has created a new background; Mr. Forster attempts a new synthesis.

Another distinction it seems useful to make, though it is only one of degree, as the first one also may be, is that whereas Hardy, to take the extreme case, says 'This is how things happen', the newer school, including Mr. Theodore Powys, who is solving problems his own way, say, 'This is what people are like'. Thus they are concerned with a much more detailed, much more delicate and sensitive, handling of persons, a handling which is perhaps proper to an age of psycho-analysis. The extreme instance in that direction is not to be found among English novelists, and is, I need hardly say, Marcel Proust. How far we are from the old method is beautifully plain if we go back to Jane Austen. In *Northanger Abbey*, for instance, Isabella Thorpe was talking about Mr. Tilney, when 'something like a sigh escaped her'. This is how Miss Austen proceeds:

> Perhaps Catherine was wrong in not demanding the cause of that gentle emotion—but she was not experienced enough in the finesse of love, or the duties of friendship, to know when delicate raillery was properly called for, or when a confidence should be forced.

Think what chapters Proust would have needed for that, or what paragraphs it would take in Mrs. Woolf! It is not merely a difference in method, that the modern writer wishes to show all the workings of the mind, but a difference in emphasis, a turn-over in values. The mind is important because the personal relation is important. And this, too, though a stage further removed than Hardy's fatalism, is a result of the collapse of faith. When God goes, man's emotions become far more important to himself. Hardy lived when to cease to believe in a future life, with its accompanying redemption and rewards to balance the ills of the present one, was still a shock. He made tragedy out of the shock: Mr. Kipling, as it were, hit back. But now, not to have that belief is no longer a shock. We have got used to it; some of us even rather like the idea. But being less important than ever in the scheme of things has made us all the more important to ourselves. We are forced to know about ourselves, and have got to make up our minds about what is worth while within the limits of mortal life.

Thus, and here is the final distinction I shall make, the new school of novelists (and this division will include the still younger people, such as Mr. David Garnett) do not judge; they definitely use their works to explore life with. This is all to the good. They do not pontificate, and do not so much seem to tell us what they find out, as to find out as they go along. It is a little bit the attitude of M. André Gide's character, who remarks, 'How can I tell what I think till I see what I say?' I do not mean that these writers literally do not know all about their works of art, or about their thoughts, just as much as the earlier ones; all I mean is that they 'take us along with them', to use the old phrase, rather than show us a panorama. And Mr. Forster, who was among the first, if he was not the first, as he may have been for all I know, to make the breakaway, exhibits this with very great clearness if we watch him at work in the order in which his novels were written.

You do definitely feel, as you read his first, *Where Angels Fear to Tread*, that here is something new, that here is somebody with an interesting and original mind working out a problem which is important to us as well as to himself. At the same time, the problem is expressed and worked out in terms of art; it is only in the form of art that such a problem could be tackled and yet retain its reality. It is, as I have hinted, the question of the 'personal relation'; and according to Mr. Forster, it is only in the novel that its difficulty can be got over. In his case, the work of art is the satisfaction of an impulse, as all good art must be.

For human intercourse [he writes in his *Aspects of the Novel*, a book second in that realm only to Mr. Percy Lubbock's *The Craft of Fiction*], as soon as we look at it for its own sake and not as a social adjunct, is seen to be haunted by a spectre. We cannot understand each other, except in a rough and ready way; we cannot reveal ourselves, even when we want to; what we call intimacy is only a makeshift; perfect knowledge is an illusion. But in the novel we can know people perfectly. . . .

That is a clear statement: it shows us both what problem Mr. Forster is trying to solve in life, and what problem he is trying to solve in the novel. He is endeavouring in his fiction to create a realm where he will not be haunted by the spectre of imperfect human relations. It is, indeed, an illuminating statement as far as it goes, but when we examine it more closely we see that it does not go very far. For the people whom we know so perfectly in novels, we only know with respect to the circumstances the novelist has carefully chosen for them. Even Clarissa Harlowe, whom I suppose we know as well as anybody we have not met, only exists by virtue of certain events. We do not know what she would be like under the conditions of, say, Becky Sharp, or Evelina. She would behave differently from either, no doubt, especially from the former, but we know no more how exactly she would behave than we know how our cousin Mary would behave. We seem to know Uncle Toby and Mr. Shandy pretty well, I suspect more intimately than any one we know in real life, but even them we do not know perfectly. Let somebody invent a situation for Uncle Toby, and ask Mr. Forster and Mrs. Woolf to describe the result; will it be the same even with authors so alike in many respects, with sensibilities and intuitions which belong to the same group? One would lay heavy odds that it will not be the same. The light really does begin to grow dim when we approach the question of intimacy, and the whole point of Mr. Forster is, ultimately, in what he conceives intimacy ought to give. I must state that I do not propose to discuss at any length the possible ultimate value of this search after the 'personal relation'. It is not at all sure whether it is the most important thing in life; it may be that to 'know thyself' is far better than to act as a sort of negative or positive pole for somebody else, so that some spark or other may fly. But at all events it is clearly excellent that good minds should embark upon a research of this sort; but it is equally clear that with bad minds, and some have attempted it, it merely becomes a rather unpleasant kind of gossip; and revealing oneself 'even when one wants to' (which apparently is pretty often) turns out to be a flabby form of confession extremely bad for anybody's character. In any final valuation of Mr. Forster's work this might have to be taken into account; for though it is still true that what matters in art is not the subject so much as the way the artist treats it (or, to put it differently, what he brings to it), unless the material is of permanent value in the human make-up, the art will be of the lesser kind.

It will readily be granted, I think, that no two more different writers than Mr. Kipling and Mr. Forster can be imagined. But it is their very opposition which shows that the insistent thought which causes each to write has its source in the same problem. We go back to Arjuna and Krishna, to the problem as to whether the life of action or the contemplative life be the better choice. We have seen Mr. Kipling's answer. Mr. Forster's answer is the contrary one. For him the life of action is a life of 'telegrams and anger', of deliberately funking the emotions of which the 'inner life' is made up. The outer life of telegrams and anger, of doing things, of making motor-cars, and roads, and Empires, destroys the best of the human impulses, charity, understanding, and respect of persons. It involves a cramping submission to social conventions, a humiliating kow-towing to Mrs. Grundy, a substitution of materialistic morality for the better morality of the spirit. It destroys, in fact, not passion, but love, which may involve passion; and love is the only creation man has to his credit.

> It will survive at the end of things, and be gathered by Fate as a jewel from the slime, and be handed with admiration round the assembly of the gods. 'Men did produce this,' they will say, and saying, they will give men immortality.

It is, in fact, the only reality, the only thing of which man can be sure. But it has implications. To say, 'The only things we can be sure of are our emotions', is too shallow and immature philosophy to appeal to Mr. Forster. Love is not only passionate desire. 'Far more mysterious than the call of sex to sex,' Mr. Forster explains, 'is the tenderness that we throw into that call;' and again, he would have us understand by love 'the various upliftings of the spirit, such as affection, friendship, patriotism, mysticism'. Thus love, besides being the 'real' thing above all others, is also a reaching out into the unseen, an attempt to extend the limits of personality, to break out of the box of the ego, to other realities than those recognized in the life of telegrams and anger.

But now that we are on this ground, what is reality? It is, perhaps, like Ibsen's Boyg, something vast, shifty, at once palpable and impalpable. 'What is reality?' is perhaps the Sphinx's riddle. It is one which has certainly much occupied Mr. Forster. This is the beginning of his second novel, *The Longest Journey*:

'The cow is there,' said Ansell, lighting a match and holding it out over the carpet. No one spoke. He waited till the end of the match fell off. Then he said again, 'She is there, the cow. There, now.'

'You have not proved it,' said a voice.

'I have proved it to myself.'

'I have proved it to myself that she isn't,' said the voice. 'The cow is *not* there.' Ansell frowned and lit another match.

'She's there for me,' he declared. 'I don't care whether she's there for you or not. Whether I'm in Cambridge or Iceland or dead, the cow will be there.'

It was, as Mr. Forster explains, philosophy, being discussed by a group of undergraduates; and the whole book is a development of the theme, or rather of the one touched upon at the end of the chapter:

Rickie spoke again, but received no answer. He paced a little up and down the sombre room. Then he sat on the edge of the table and watched his clever friend draw within [a] square a circle, and within the circle a square, and inside that another circle, and inside that another square.

'Why will you do that?'

No answer.

'Are they real?'

'The inside one is—the one in the middle of everything, that there's never room enough to draw.

The real thing, then, is the unseen; but it does not follow that because it is unseen, it is any the less potent.

We may, within discreet limits, take *The Longest Journey* as in a sense autobiographical, since one of the stories written by the hero of the book is the same as one Mr. Forster himself wrote in that delightful volume of fantasy, *The Celestial Omnibus*. In fantasy, we think, the supernatural has the same value as the solid, as far as counters go. 'Why place an angel on a different basis from a stockbroker?' so, according to Mr. Forster, we say. 'Once in the realm of the fictitious, what difference is there between an apparition and a mortgage?' But still, there is that extra little twist, and Mr. Forster denies himself the advantage of being able to make use of it when he writes the full-length novel. Nevertheless, for him, as for his hero, the unseen is there.

It is there even in his first novel, *Where Angels Fear to Tread*, which, though quite traditional in form, cries aloud in every page that here is an individual mind working. The story is the regrettable one of a girl who married into a suburb she did not quite fit. She was never beyond question 'one of us', though she was skilfully made to conform outwardly to sound standards. She became a widow, and then made a fatal journey to Italy. There she married on impulse, under the witchery of Southern skies, not only an Italian, but a dentist, and went to live in a house with a deplorable drainage system. She dies, and her son is accidentally killed while being kidnapped by its righteously indignant English relatives, who want to make the infant safe for respectability. Two worlds are opposed, the world of convention of the seen, and the world of impulse and the unseen. Which is the stronger? There is no doubt. But which is the brighter? Again there is no doubt, in spite of misery, and death, and a deplorable drainage system. The life of impulse was at least once alive, that of convention always dead; the former contained material for art, which is a living thing; the latter only the materials for culture, which is a dead thing. The same theme is worked out in Mr. Forster's third novel, *A Room With a View*.

In his next book, *Howards End*, the subject is still treated, but it is only a part of the theme, which is now broadened to include the opposite point of view. 'Only connect' was the epigraph to the first edition of that book, that is, only connect the inner life with the outer, and then you will be able to see life steadily and see it whole. But do not, even if you acknowledge the virtues of the life of action, neglect 'the impact of the unseen upon the seen'. It is only by a fusion of the two points of view that life can become a reasonable whole.

The person in this novel who tries to unite the two is Margaret Schlegel; the extreme idealist, her sister Helen; while the opposite camp is represented by the Wilcoxes, a successful business family. But over both groups there hovers the spirit of the late Mrs. Wilcox, who seemed to have been able to connect by sheer affection, and by doing nothing. All the actions of the living seem to weave themselves into the pattern she wanted, so much so that Margaret says at one time:

I feel that you and I and Henry [Wilcox] are only fragments of that woman's mind. She knows everything. She is everything. . . . I cannot believe that knowledge such as hers will perish with knowledge such as mine. She knew about realities. She knew when people were in love, though she was not in the room.

She is the sage, and she recurs as Mrs. Moore in Mr. Forster's last novel, *A Passage to India*. I have brought in the older Mrs. Wilcox as a gloss on the Helen Schlegel standpoint, because Margaret's attitude towards her is an expression of something which figures large in modern literature, a sort of inverted Berkeleyism which one might call Pirandellism. It is on the conception of our existing only in other people's minds that Signor Pirandello's best-known plays are built. A reference to it in this book is no mere accident, for it recurs in *A Passage to India*. Speaking of one of the characters in that courageous novel, he says:

> And fatigued by the merciless and enormous day, he lost his usual sane view of human intercourse, and felt that we exist, not in ourselves, but in terms of each others' minds—a notion for which logic offers no support. . . .

We begin to suspect that too much brooding over the personal relation must inevitably lead to this, which is in the end but a renunciation of individuality, a weak giving up of the sense of personal responsibility. It is a form of what Coleridge called 'the thinking disease', namely,

> that in which the feelings, instead of embodying themselves in acts, ascend, and become materials of general reasoning and intellectual pride . . . *feelings* made the subjects and tangible substance of thought, instead of actions, realizations, *things done*. . . . On such meagre diet as feelings, evaporated embryos in their progress to *birth*, no moral beings ever become healthy.

Mr. Kipling, and perhaps Aristotle, would applaud that doctrine. Mr. Forster is not so sure; he has seen too much of the opposite extreme, action which is merely an excuse for not thinking, an evasion of emotion due to muddled thought. He really endorses Mr. Kipling's view that

> the everyday affair of business, meals and clothing,
> Builds a Bulkhead 'twixt Despair, and the Edge of Nothing,

since he believes that it is precisely the people who live on the edge of nothing, and whose background is chaos and darkness, that take refuge in the life of action. Yet he does not deny the use of action; it makes for surety, for stability, for comfort; it supplies, for those who can use it, that leisure without which the inner life cannot exist at all. He is less panic-stricken than Mr. Kipling, and, unlike him, can see not only the opposition between the views discussed by Krishna and Arjuna, but a possible balance. 'Only connect,' he says, which Mr. Kipling refuses to attempt, if only for a moment. But even the upholder of the inner life must see the value of the outer life. Helen Schlegel says to Margaret:

> You and I have built up something real, because it is purely spiritual. There is no veil of mystery over us. Unreality and mystery begin as soon as one touches the body. The popular view is, as usual, the wrong one. Our bothers are over tangible things— money, husbands, house-hunting. But heaven will work of itself.
>
> Margaret was grateful for this expression of affection, and answered 'Perhaps'. All vistas close in the unseen—no one doubts it—but Helen closed them rather too quickly for her taste. At every turn of speech one was confronted with reality and the absolute. . . . She felt there was something a little unbalanced in the mind that so readily shreds the visible.

Proportion, the old healer, may still have its value to-day.

I do not wish to suggest that Mr. Forster's novels read like metaphysical disquisitions; his is the method of the artist, and so far we have only touched upon the materials peculiar to him, the intuitions which he brings to the facts of life. His novels are objects in themselves, his people distinctive people. It is true that those whom he dislikes are apt to be 'humours', flat figures, as he would say, and not figures in the round. But there is not necessarily any harm in that, especially where comedy is aimed at, even in a novel. For if Ben Jonson's figures are flat, so are most of Dickens's; we know them only by a few attributes. And throughout Mr. Forster's flat figures, or rather, implicit in their movements, there runs a delightful irony, not a second-rate one suggesting a contempt of mankind; it is rather because he finds mankind valuable that he has it there. Indeed, his is an elfin irony which enlivens without hurting, in spite of an element of satire. Those who know that bundle of enchanting essays on Egypt, *Pharos and Pharillon*, or the guide-book to Alexandria—surely the best guide-book ever written—will be familiar with this aspect of him. It is the demure seriousness with which he slips in the deftly satirical remark that makes it ludicrous. Take this from a novel, for instance: 'She might have seen a flash of horror pass over Rickie's face. The horror disappeared, for, thank God, he was now a man, whom civilization protects,' from, of course, his emotions. Or, of those women who look after the obvious comforts of under-graduates in our senior universities: 'Bedmakers have to be comic and dishonest. It is expected of them. In a picture of university life, it is their only function.' Or we read of Sir Gilbert Mellanby, who, 'though not an enlightened man, held enlightened opinions'. His work is full of such touches, and his attacks always seem to wear a look of innocence upon their faces. Here, for instance, is how he lodges an arrow in 'culture', that blight of art, and in those who ensue it. A young woman has gone to Santa Croce, armed with Baedeker, and hortatory texts from Ruskin. 'Then the pernicious charm of Italy worked on her, and, instead of acquiring information, she began to be happy.' But let us take one of his longer passages, one about that admirable figure in *The Longest Journey*, Mr. Pembroke, who teaches at one of those schools recognized as pillars of the Empire, which, originally founded for the children of the poor, now open their portals only to the sons of the rich:

Here Mr. Pembroke passed his happy and industrious life. His

technical position was that of master to a form low down on the
Modern Side. But his work lay elsewhere. He organized. If no
organization existed, he would create one. If one did exist, he
would modify it. 'An organization', he would say, 'is, after all, not
an end in itself. It must contribute to a movement.' When one
good custom seemed likely to corrupt the school, he was ready with
another; he believed that without innumerable customs there was
no safety, either for boy or man. Perhaps he is right, and always
will be right. Perhaps each of us would go to ruin if for one short
hour we acted as we thought fit, and attempted the service of perfect
freedom. The school caps, with their elaborate symbolism, were
his; his the many-tinted bathing-drawers, that showed how far a
boy could swim; his the hierarchy of jerseys and blazers. It was he
who instituted Bounds, and Call, and the three sorts of caning, and
'The Sawstonian', a bi-terminal magazine. His plump finger was in
every pie. The dome of his skull, mild but impressive, shone at
every masters' meeting. He was generally acknowledged to be the
coming man.

It will be seen that Mr. Forster likes to interpolate the
comment, so as to make a general truth out of the particular truth he is putting before us. This is, in the main,
a reprehensible practice, as it takes us out of the world of
fiction into our own world; it snaps the thread which
connects us with the characters of the story, and is apt to
give us a snobbish feeling of superiority over them.
Thackeray is a prime sinner in this respect, and when at the
end of *Vanity Fair* he tells us to put away the puppets and
shut up the box because the play is played out, we begin to
think that after all Rawdon Crawley and Sir Pitt, Amelia
and Becky, not to mention the battle of Waterloo, are of
very small moment indeed. But somehow, when Mr.
Forster stands aside from his characters, he produces a
different effect; he does not seem to say, 'Look how little
all this matters!' but rather, 'Now, look here; don't you
realize that you too are involved? Can't you see how
important this is to you, as well as to these people I am
showing you?' The comment is part of his search, and he
'takes us along with him' in it. By this means he creates a

7

feeling of extraordinary intimacy with his characters; we not only share their outward life, as we do that of Tom Jones or Quentin Durward, but we partake of their secret life as well. We cannot help becoming excited, not so much at what these people do, as at what they are. It becomes of great account that so and so should behave like this or that. I know of no other novelist who gives just this quality of excitement. It is not so much that we want to know what will happen next, as we do in a novel by Mr. Edgar Wallace, as that we like to stay with the characters at the critical moment of their lives. We feel that when any of the people we like score, we score too: when they fail, the failure is ours. The story does not really matter to us any more than it does to Mr. Forster; to tell a tale is not the object of a novel. He will say, not vaguely and good-temperedly, not briskly nor aggressively, but a little sadly, 'Yes—oh dear yes—the novel tells a story.' But it is only the scaffolding, not the substance. The story exists merely to put the people in play, so that we may know them perfectly, more perfectly than we can know any one in real life.

At the same time, though we do passionately take sides in reading Mr. Forster's novels, there is yet another quality to be noted in him, and that in his scrupulous fairness. I do not say his impartiality, but his fairness, for he is not impartial. Not that he is always quite successful in being fair, for complete fairness is a divine attribute; but his effort to be fair is remarkable. Even when he is exhibiting something unpleasant in a character whom he does not like, some deadness of sensibility inherent in the man of action, for instance, we hear a voice whispering 'Only connect', or 'See life steadily and see it whole'. And in no book of his does this desire for fairness come out so clearly as in *A Passage to India*. It is not, of course, quite fair, because the people he dislikes are still in the flat. They achieve the social emotions, but refuse to face the personal ones, while the people he likes achieve both. In this novel he even goes so far as to seem to doubt the value of the personal relation. Mrs. Moore, for instance, 'felt increasingly (vision or nightmare?) that, though people are important, the relations between them are not'. Or again:

'I shall not really be intimate with this fellow,' Fielding thought, and then, 'nor with anyone.' That was the corollary. And he had to confess that he really didn't mind, that he was content to help people, and like them as long as they didn't object, and if they objected, pass on serenely. Experience can do much, and all that he had learnt in England and Europe was an assistance to him, and helped him towards clarity, but clarity prevented him from experiencing something else.

Is then the personal relation as much a product of muddle as the life of telegrams and anger? Is there, perhaps, panic and emptiness behind both of them? 'No,' Mr. Forster will answer: 'it is true that the personal relation is not quite the universal panacea I once thought it was, but there is something else.' This something else is only indicated, and a little vaguely at that; it is a life force, and a kindly life force, if not so rich as Tolstoy's, yet not so grim as Hardy's. You feel it when you read his moving description of England seen from the final section of the Purbeck Hills, when in the evening she 'becomes alive, throbbing through all her estuaries, crying for joy through the mouth of her gulls'. You feel it in the brilliant phantasmogoria of a Hindu festival, where even the ridiculous figure of Professor Godbole, his face smeared over with butter, and dancing before the god, takes on something of the divine. What does it all mean? How can one connect the Isle of Wight with mankind, the West with the East? For this latter is the problem of *A Passage to India*. Mr. Kipling says they meet when two strong men stand face to face, but Mr. Forster does not like strong men. Yet the personal relation will not do; the earth and the rocks, the temples and the tanks of India say 'No, not yet', and the sky says, 'No, not there'. What then? There is only one cure, and it is a very slow one; it is kindness, and more kindness, and again kindness. Emotion is still the important thing; it is still in the end, the earth that must win, just as it is the earth which wins in *The Longest Journey* in the person of that strange savage, Stephen Wonham, with his picture of Demeter flapping in the wind. It is, no doubt, a lesson that the world must learn, and that we all of us should learn, namely, that it is the mother passions which count; though most of us, like King Lear, learn it too late. Still, the question arises, were there no conflict, would life be worth living? Probably not; not because conflict is in itself exhilarating (some like it better than others), but because without conflict there can be no values. 'Without opposition', Blake said, 'there can be no progression.'

If, to conclude, we hazard a valuation of Mr. Forster's work, if we try to decide whether what he has to say be a lasting and important contribution to the sort of 'truth' to which mankind will return, we must make a modest claim; and I do not think that Mr. Forster would wish for any other. His work will always have vividness, charm, and distinction; it will always be indubitably his. But that is just where the criticism lies; it has not quite that authority of 'anonymity' which he himself declares to be the hallmark of the greatest work. Anybody could have written *Homer*, or *Macbeth*, or *War and Peace*, 'if he had had the mind to'; but only Mr. Forster could have written *Howards End*. The truth is, that like Mrs. Woolf, though not to the same degree, he has written of what, in humanity, lies between the notable points. It is worth doing, and he has done it extremely well. But the doubt creeps in; can you really give, or re-create, the 'personal relation', the 'inner life' in this way? They are rather, like those unpursuable things, beauty and happiness; and of beauty he himself has written, in one of those acute and memorable *obiter dicta* with which his work is spangled, that in a novel beauty is part of a completed plot:

> She looks a little surprised at being there, but beauty ought to look a little surprised; it is the emotion that best suits her face, as Boticelli knew when he painted her risen from the waves, between the winds and the flowers. The beauty who does not look surprised, who accepts her position as her due—she reminds us too much of a prima donna.

Perhaps in the same way, the personal relation is part of a completed life, and should look a little surprised at being there. If it accepts its position as its due—it reminds us too much of a war memorial. But Mr. Forster's touch is too light to make us feel that; he would not commit that sort of artistic blunder, or crush a butterfly upon a wheel. And at least, and it is a big least, in a civilization which is growing at once more complex and more standardized, he is keeping open a door which it would be very dreary indeed, and very perilous, to have forever inexorably shut.

D. H. LAWRENCE

THERE is no living writer who is at once so seductive and so aggravating as Mr. Lawrence. He is a man of genius who continually and wilfully denies his genius, partly through revulsion against the professional side of writing, a holy horror of becoming an *homme du métier*; and partly through desire to propagate his faith. A brilliant writer of descriptive prose, with a rhythm as potent as that of de Quincey when he cares to use it, and a command of the right word and metaphor which is given to very few, he despises fine writing even where it would best serve his purpose. It is as though born an artist, and desiring to be a priest, he is afraid that his art will get the better of him; and where there is fear, there cannot be the complete control of material essential to great art. His genius, therefore, is of the fiery sort now leaping into plumes of flame, now sinking into a sultry glow: it is not of the order which reveals itself in clear lightning flashes illuminating the surroundings. Consequently there is often much smoke, and sometimes confusion.

There is, then, hardly any book of Mr. Lawrence's which one does not read with mingled feelings of delight and anger; but if one is wise, one will allow the anger to evaporate, and the delight to be renewed. At least he is original, not in any silly way of form devoid of a complementary content, but in what he has progressively tried to do, from his earlier books and his first poems, where one is already immediately sensible of power, to his later work. Where he is at his best is in his purely descriptive passages, not only in books of such, but also in his novels and stories, because there neither his desperate attempt to find a direct equivalence between thought and sensation where none can exist, nor his urgency to inculcate a doctrine, can break in to spoil the integrity of the thing made. He can give, incomparably, the actuality of a thing, making it more real than reality, not by any forced means, or titanic tricks of language often resorted to by modern writers, but by new metaphor, which is the poetic means of creation. He does not use the ready-made, deadening words. Take, for instance, the phrase 'the upright morning'; there is in it an unexpected wedding of two words, a uniting of attributes which produces a new meaning, that is to say, a new thing, which is at once accepted. It is by the use of such phrases that a language is kept expressively alive, and the born writer reveals himself. Moreover he is wonderfully sensitive to the feel of things, to their aspects and relations, so that his descriptions do not remain as mere descriptions, useful settings, but become poetic objects in themselves.

It was a magnificent morning in early spring when I watched among the trees to see the procession come down the hillside. The upper air was woven with the music of the larks, and my whole world thrilled with the conception of summer. The young pale wind-flowers had arisen by the woodgale, and under the hazels; when perchance the hot sun pushed his way, new little suns dawned, and blazed with real light. There was a certain thrill and quickening everywhere, as a woman must feel when she has conceived. A sallow tree in a favoured spot looked like a pale gold cloud of summer down; nearer it had poised a golden, fairy busby on every twig, and was voiced with a hum of bees, like any sacred golden bush, uttering its gladness in the sacred murmur of bees, and in warm scent. Birds called and flashed on every hand; they made off exultant with streaming strands of grass, or wisps of fleece, plunging into the dark spaces of the wood, and out again into the blue.

(From *The White Peacock*)

It may be objected that such passages, and even so splendid a one is from an earlier novel, no doubt do very well to make up a volume of descriptive essays, and there are indeed some who prefer such things as *Sea and Sardinia* and *Mornings in Mexico* to his other work; but, they would argue, such description is only a small portion of the novelist's task, and the test must come when considering Mr. Lawrence as a novelist, as to whether he can apply the same method to people, to make them at once so alive and so solid. Here, as a proof, is a short passage from *Twilight in Italy*, which is not a novel:

> Her fingers worked away all the time in a little, half-fretful movement, yet spontaneous as butterflies leaping here and there. She chattered rapidly on in her Italian that I could not understand, looking meanwhile into my face, because the story roused her somewhat. Yet not a feature moved. Her eyes remained candid and open and unconscious as the skies. Only a sharp will in them now and then seemed to gleam at me, as if to dominate me.
>
> Her shuttle had caught in a dead chicory plant, and spun no more. She did not notice. I stooped and broke off the twigs. There was a glint of blue on them yet. Seeing what I was doing, she merely withdrew a few inches from the plant. Her bobbin hung free.
>
> She went on with her tale, looking at me wonderfully. She seemed like the Creation, like the beginning of the world, the first morning. Her eyes were like the first morning of the world, so ageless.
>
> Her thread broke. She seemed to take no notice, but mechanically picked up the shuttle, wound up a length of worsted, connected the ends from her wool strand, set the bobbin spinning again, and went on talking, in her half-intimate, half-unconscious fashion, as if she were talking to her own world in me.
>
> So she stood in the sunshine on the little platform, old and yet like the morning, erect and solitary, sun-coloured, sun-discoloured, whilst I at her elbow, like a piece of night and moonshine, stood smiling into her eyes, afraid lest she should deny me existence.
>
> Which she did. . . .

Those extracts are enough to show the quality of Mr. Lawrence's pen, but except for their energy, for their fine sensitiveness, they do not differentiate him from any other traditional writer. And it may well be insisted here that he does indeed possess that energy without which no great writing can be done, and that he is a traditional writer in that he is concerned with the broad flow of human life. He is not like some excellent modern authors, who are adding maybe some small thread to the fabric of literature, exquisitely exploring only some corner of sensibility, or working out some purely literary problem. It is from a traditional ground that he is enlarging the scope of the novel; and it is only in enlarging the scope of the novel, in being different from other novelists, that his problem arises: what precisely his problem is will be discussed in a moment.

First we must turn to his conception of the function of the novel, and this is explicitly stated in his latest work, *Lady Chatterley's Lover*:

It is the way our sympathy flows and recoils that really determines our lives. And here lies the vast importance of the novel, properly handled. It can inform and lead into new places the flow of our sympathetic consciousness, and it can lead our sympathy away in recoil from things gone dead. Therefore, the novel, properly handled, can reveal the most secret places of life: for it is in the *passional* secret places of life, above all, that the tide of sensitive awareness needs to ebb and flow, cleansing and freshening.

It is not much to go on by itself, except to separate Mr. Lawrence from the novelists who wish to crystallize life; but taken in connexion with the general trend of his development, it serves to illuminate his writing to more than a small degree. The thing with which he means his readers to get contact, this tide of sensitive awareness, is some, to us dimly, to him vividly apprehended, large flow of life; not social or personal adjustment, but some rhythmic pulse beating at the base of things. Mr. Lawrence, then, is a mystic, though not one of the namby-pamby, peaky-faced variety; nor does he belong to the solemn mouthing crew of the would-be God-intoxicated. His is a robust religion, to be reached only through an intense appreciation of the physical, especially of the sexual. The religion of which he is priest and prophet is a phallic one. To some it seems as though he were imbued with a magnificent and glorying sensuality, but although this is true, it is not the whole of the truth. And the qualification rests, not, as might occasionally appear, in that some demon of puritanism every now and then points a finger to reveal the skeleton beneath the perfumed flesh, but that he knows the senses can never be satisfied, and that he seeks some ultimate end. His is an ethical, almost a metaphysical search; and in so far as he will not accept the limitations of humanity, he is a romantic. Moreover, he is profoundly dissatisfied with the complexion life wears to-day. He regards modern love with horror; it seems to him to lack real springs, to be devoid of the satisfaction of something which is more primitive than the physical, and which, for want of a better word, might be called the impulsive. He despises lust as much as he does the intellectualized or spiritualized love affair: he sees man sapped by futile love as well as by futile hatred and spite. His propagandist nature, then, for he has a propagandist nature, is bent towards bringing men back to a realization of impulsive being.

To do this he has to improve upon, and give significance to, physical experience. But first the physical experience has to be fully and vividly realized: and to make this actual, to find words to describe not only physical sensation, but the emotional reflexes accompanying it, is his literary problem. Moreover, what he has tried to do, sometimes with disastrous results, is to find the equivalent of the deeper emotional feelings in physical sensation: his readers are only too familiar with persons who go black inside. One small, and not altogether unsuccessful passage, from the story 'Sun', in the volume *The Woman Who Rode Away*, may serve as an example. He is describing a woman sun-bathing:

She could feel the sun penetrating even into her bones ; nay, further, even into her emotions and her thoughts. The dark tensions of her emotion began to give way, the cold dark clots of her thoughts began to dissolve. She was beginning to feel warm right through. Turning over, she let her shoulders dissolve in the sun, her loins, the backs of her thighs, even her heels. And she lay half stunned with wonder at the thing that was happening to her. Her weary, chilled heart was melting, and, in melting, evaporating.

So far good; but that is not enough for Mr. Lawrence, and in a later passage we read:

It was not just taking sunbaths. It was much more than that. Some thing deep inside her unfolded and relaxed, and she was given. By some mysterious power inside her, deeper than her known consciousness and will, she was put into connection with the sun, and the stream flowed of itself from her womb. She herself, her conscious self, was secondary, a secondary person, almost an onlooker. The true Juliet was this dark flow from her deep body to the sun.

Something, we feel, is being strained; note 'the *dark* flow', 'her *deep* body': Mr. Lawrence is trying to make prose do something that prose cannot do, namely describe direct sensation. You cannot describe direct sensation: try to describe sweetness, and you will fail. Some things have to be taken for granted as the common feeling of humanity. There are places beyond which words cannot go, but this Mr. Lawrence refuses to admit, and it is his struggle to force words beyond their function which sometimes distresses his readers.

There are other results of Mr. Lawrence's desire to pierce deeper than consciousness, or even than subconsciousness in the ordinary sense, the most notable of which is his love of the more earthy man as opposed to the cultured one, which in some of his later phases has driven him back to the more primitive races, notably the Mexican Indians, since it is those whom he has known. This has earned him a diatribe from Mr. Wyndham Lewis for being a renegade from thought, a flinger-away of the guards mankind has raised against savagery, as one who fleeing from the complex issues of modernity, surrenders the struggle of civilization. But if Mr. Lawrence mocks at the cultured man, it is for his thinness of apprehension, his poor assumptions and his conceit, because he feels in him a loss of power through a loss of contact with nature. He is like an apple plucked away from the parent tree; there is nothing for him, but to rot. And if there is a back to the land, back to the savage element in Mr. Lawrence, it is only an element, or perhaps not even that, merely a symbolism; it is not altogether sentimental, and by no means a form of Rousseauism. For him the savage is not noble because he is pure and simple, childlike, and perhaps a vegetarian, but precisely because he is savage, and has mystic apprehensions of being, of blood, of fibre and fire, which the cultivated man has carefully eliminated. His is not so much a plea for savagery, as an onslaught upon tye mental life. And certainly, knowing as he does the kind of people who lead the so-called mental life, one can to a large extent sympathize with Mr. Lawrence. His attack is upon the aridity and tenuousness of the mental livers, their distortion of the passionate life, and he pleads for a return to a more natural habit of living which will pay some heed to the mystic implications of being as being. This attitude has been latent in his work from the first, whether in his early novels, his poems, or his plays, or that admirable piece of criticism *American Classical Literature*, which is the best book on the subject so far written. His theme, however, is stated fully in his later work, such as *The Plumed Serpent*, some of his short stories, and especially in *Lady Chatterley's Lover*, in which he has thrown all drawing-room decorum to the winds, applying to cultivated life the principles of *The Plumed Serpent*, which relates a primitive revivalist movement among Mexicans. The result of this application is not altogether satisfactory, and it is not certain that Mr. Lawrence has avoided destroying just what he most wanted to preserve, integrity of impulse. For just as too rigorous an intellectual analysis has, in his view, deadened the magic of love, so too acute a description of sensation, however glamorously worded, may annihilate that magic. It is, perhaps, possible to arrive through sheer sensuality at something beyond, at a vision of beauty too fragile to possess, as Keats sometimes did in his poetry, as occasionally an ancient Egyptian sculptor succeeded in doing; but it will not be done by trying to repiece the shattered physical into some intellectual pattern, however 'cosmic' its intention. And here some words of Landor may be applicable:

From the mysteries of religion the veil is seldom to be drawn, from the mysteries of love, never. For this offence the gods take away from us freshness of heart and our susceptibility of pure delight. The well loses the springs that fed it, and what is exposed in the shallow basin soon evaporates.

According to some, maybe, as to one of his own characters, it is as well that it should evaporate; but it is the last thing Mr. Lawrence desires.

What it is that Mr. Lawrence looks for to revivify a wearied generation is, then, a kind of phallic mysticism; not, as already said, any high-falutin' mysticism, but one of the flesh. Inspired by his genius, made alive by his immense literary talent for causing a thing to exist, his vision is momentarily exciting, and even, at moments, plausible. As a criticism of the enfeebled emotional life which drags on in most great cities, it has a deal of point. It could be expressed in terms of later Greek mythology, but without that regrettable flippancy so often shown by members of the Greek Pantheon, without the Attic balance, without, should one say, the Attic sense of humour. Yet really Mr. Lawrence delves further back into ethnology, to a time before the sun could be viewed in the charming lineaments of Apollo, or the moon in the delightful graces of Artemis. We are back to something more primitive, when the sun devours, the moon has sway over the waters, and the serpent is felt crawling in the bosom of the earth. He found a satisfying solution in the old Mexican religion, a solution which, as we shall see, altered the angle of his vision. To put it very crudely and broadly, he has found symbols adequate to his intuition in a marriage of the sun and moon, which marriage produced offspring in the earth's gods or prophets, who in turn animate men, the issue of the earth-serpent. It has, naturally, more subtle and complicated ramifications, which are, moreover, clothed in splendour by the art of a powerful writer.

Why such a symbolism should satisfy so modern an author as Mr. Lawrence is apparent on reading his other novels. For however much he may be telling a story, or presenting the life of to-day, there is one theme which more and more dominates his writing—and that is the relation, not so much of the sexes, that poor over-battered theme, but of the male and female principles. For him there is somewhere essential maleness, and somewhere else essential femaleness, both, of course, necessary to universal fruition. But everywhere in men he sees a lack of real virility, and in women of real femineity: all has been distorted by consciousness, by religions, by over-intellectualization. Instead of leading the life of impulse, men and women lead lives directed at one extreme by the body, at the other by the mind: men are devoted to absurd schemes of power or position, or to mere money-grubbing. Everywhere people are worshipping false gods, involved in spiteful partisanships, or wasteful snobberies. What appealed to him in the Mexicans was their dogged opposition to the spirit, their refusal to rationalize away their hatred or their jealousies, or to abandon their brooding for the occidental lust after movement; but above all he loved them for keeping something secret and reserved in themselves. This is a passage from *The Plumed Serpent*:

But Kate, standing back in the doorway, with Juana sitting on the doorstep at her feet, was fascinated by the silent, half-naked ring of men in the torchlight. Their heads were black, their bodies soft and ruddy with the peculiar Indian beauty that has at the same time something terrible in it. The soft, full, handsome torsos of silent men with heads softly bent a little forward; the soft, easy shoulders that are yet so broad, and which balance upon so powerful a backbone; shoulders drooping a little, with the relaxation of slumbering, quiescent power; the beautiful ruddy skin, gleaming with a dark fineness; the strong breasts, so male and so deep, yet without the muscular hardening that belongs to white men; and the dark, closed faces, closed upon a darkened consciousness, the black moustaches, and delicate beards framing the closed silence of the mouth; all this was strangely impressive, moving strange, frightening emotions in the soul. The men who sat there in their dark, physical tenderness, so still and soft, they looked at the same time frightening. Something dark, heavy, and reptilian in their silence and their softness. Their very naked torsos were clothed with a subtle shadow, a certain secret obscurity. White men sitting there would have been strong-muscled and frank, with an openness in their very physique, a certain ostensible presence. But not so these men. Their very nakedness only revealed the soft, heavy depths of their natural secrecy, their eternal invisibility. They did not belong to the realm of that which comes forth.

It is precisely this core of individuality which Mr. Lawrence finds wanting in the modern man, the cultivated man, with his 'ostensible presence'. The result is that he does not act with his whole self. It is thus that the passionate life becomes distorted; pure maleness and pure femaleness are lost. Men and women cannot meet each other each on their own ground: they are involved in a continual conflict, a battering and tearing of each other, a devouring of each other, a universal clapper-clawing. Mr. Lawrence re-states, with profounder implications, the old story of sex-antagonism, which is not the same thing as the complementary opposition of the sexes. And here we

come to the curious change his views seem to have undergone since writing *The Plumed Serpent*. Whereas before,
sometimes implied, sometimes stated directly, he conceived of woman as the destroyer of man's work, continually undermining his integrity, spoiling his directness,
binding him in chains; now it appears that it is the fault
of man, who has gone astray after temporal gods instead of
hearkening to the eternal voice of the divine impulse.
Something has gone wrong with the inner balance. 'If
women are thieves, it is only because men want to be
thieved from. If women thieve the world's virility, it is
only because men want to have it thieved, since for men to
be responsible for their own manhood seems to be the last
thing men want.' Thus there is always snatching and being
stolen from, further distortion of the personality. But
under proper conditions:

> There is no giving and no taking. When the fingers that give
> touch the fingers that receive, the Morning Star shines at once, from
> the contact, and the jasmine gleams between the hands. And thus
> there is neither giving nor taking, nor hand that proffers nor hand
> that receives, but the star between them is all, and the dark hand
> and the light hand are invisible on each side. The jasmine takes the
> giving and the receiving in her cup, and the scent of the oneness is
> fragrant on the air.

Thus what causes Mr. Lawrence's deep concern is the
mal-adjustments of life, the suppressions, the deformities:
his distinctive material is really the same as that of
Dr. Freud, and the modern psycho-analytical school.

It may have been noticed that the idea of oneness stated
in the passage just quoted seems to contradict the doctrine
of sex polarity referred to earlier. But this is not so,
because the oneness is only a momentary thing, in the
nature of an impact between two beings, who must ever
remain themselves, though not for always Mr. Kipling's
lonely selves. For Mr. Lawrence's plea, his fierce battling
(there is always an element of fierceness in everything he

writes), is for individuality as opposed to the smudginess, the universal grey, of standardized democracy, wearing the same ugly clothes, eating the same tasteless food, digesting the same newspapers. And this individuality implies a hard core of reserve, impossible under the system of 'personal relations' expounded by Mr. Forster. Let me quote a passage from *Sea and Sardinia*, which illustrates not only this point, but Mr. Lawrence's more pugilistic style:

They are amusing, these peasant girls and women: so brisk and defiant. They have straight backs like little walls, and decided, well-drawn brows. And they are amusingly on the alert. There is no eastern creeping. Like sharp, brisk birds they dart along the streets, and you feel they would fetch you a bang over the head as lieve as look at you. Tenderness, thank heaven, does not seem to be a Sardinian quality. Italy is so tender—like cooked macaroni— yards and yards of soft tenderness ravelled round everything. Here men don't idealize women, by the look of things. Here they don't make those great leering eyes, the inevitable yours-to-command look of Italian males. When the men from the country look at these women, then it is Mind-yourself, my lady. I should think the grovelling Madonna-worship is not much of a Sardinian feature. These women have to look out for themselves, keep their own backbone stiff, and their knuckles hard. Man is going to be male Lord if he can. And woman isn't going to give him too much of his own way either. So there you have it, the fine old martial split between the sexes. It is tonic and splendid really, after so much sticky intermingling and backboneless Madonna-worship. The Sardinian isn't looking for the 'noble woman nobly planned.' No, thank you. He wants that young madam over there, a young stiff-necked generation that she is. Far better sport than with the nobly planned sort: hollow frauds that they are. Better sport too than with a Carmen, who gives herself away too much. In these women there is something shy and defiant and ungetatable. The defiant splendid split between the sexes, each absolutely determined to defend his side, her side, from assault. So the meeting has a certain wild, salty savour, each the deadly unknown to each other. And at the same time, each his own, her own native pride and courage, taking the dangerous leap and scrambling back.

Give me the old, salty way of love. How I am nauseated with sentiment and nobility, the macaroni slithery-slobbery mess of modern adorations.

8

But it must not for a moment be thought that Mr. Lawrence is merely a didactic writer, that he is inculcating some life-force theory after the manner of Mr. Shaw, or tidying up the world like Mr. Wells. He is first and foremost a poet, feeling his thoughts like a poet, clothing his intuitions in the actuality of the word, and making them live in the guise of people and things. His is the revolt of the poet, not the discomfort of the social reformer; his preaching, where it occurs, is of the prophetic order, which also is a kind of poetry. What he is striving for is a unity of being, and in this he reveals himself as the typical Englishman, mistrusting logic as enemy to a completer wisdom. 'The Englishman,' Professor Madariaga writes in his illuminating book on national characteristics,

does not seem to think with his brain. His ideas are not ideas properly speaking, but opinions, sentiments, sensations. He does not say 'I think', but 'I feel'. His opinions do not seem to be emitted by his brain, but by his neck, chest, abdomen, elbows or knees. His whole body emits vitalized thought as if the thinking function in him were not concentrated in the brain, but spread uniformly all over his nervous system.

Mr. Lawrence aims at thinking with his whole body, and in this he resembles the English metaphysical poets, who were not afraid to acknowledge that feeling was itself a mode of thought. But, in case this attitude may be thought over-solemn, it must not be assumed that he is lacking in sense of humour. He is not; he abounds in delightful touches, and is often brimful of laughter, as in that delectable story 'Glad Ghosts' in the volume *The Woman Who Rode Away*. Without that he would scarcely be English.

And since he is primarily a poet, it is as a poet that he must be not only judged, but tasted and enjoyed. So considered, his work as a whole takes upon itself something of epic proportions, but it is not that which need concern us here. What is immediately interesting is the way the novel, as he conceives it, is changing under his hands. His early work, such as *Sons and Lovers*, is frankly traditional, though tinged with genius (genius is a permissible word when speaking of Mr. Lawrence), but a gradual change is perceptible through *The Lost Girl*, *Aaron's Rod*, and his other books, to his last volumes. His characters are more and more becoming embodiments of ideas; the idea comes first, and has to be clothed in flesh and blood: but it cannot be too much insisted that his ideas are not purely intellectual ones. Mr. Lawrence does not say 'I think', but 'I feel'. Thus his persons are vividly, pulsingly alive, with a vitality of their own. Yet they are becoming 'humours', in the old sense of the word, not of course the Jonsonian ones of the old comedy, but strictly Lorentian ones; and this remains true however much the mere physical likeness, or certain mental aspects, may be faithfully copied from figures in real life. For this reason again, the value of his work, its coherence, its validity within itself, must depend increasingly upon its sheer poetic quality. Poetic power is growing in him, so that, using more and more the image to represent the emotion, he need no longer so often aim at the direct description of emotion as physical sensation. Since then he is a poet, and not only in his verse, his characters and his philosophy must not be taken literally for things in themselves: they are only the symbols the poet has to use to give his intuitions body and form. Taken as bald statements, many of the things Mr. Lawrence writes may well sound ridiculous: a real belief in the Mexican mythology crudely outlined above would be merely absurd. But that is of no account in poetry, just as a real belief in Dante being guided by Virgil through the infernal regions is of no account. What does matter is the intensity with which the intuition, the symbol, and the image are welded together into one self-existing object. It might be easy to destroy Mr. Lawrence's work on philosophical, logical, common-sense, or all sorts of other grounds; but as poetry, though here and there it may fall lamentably from grace, as often as not through exaggeration, it will be found to resist a good deal of attack. There is too much stuff in it to let it fall easily.

It is luckily not the business of the critic to place his victim in some hierarchy of merit, but it is part of his job to find out to what realm he belongs, and in what current of tradition he is situated. As regards the latter, Mr. Lawrence is, it is hardly necessary to say, in the grand tradition of poetic novelists, of Emily Brontë, of Thomas Hardy, who try to seize life as a whole, rather than to analyse it or to comment upon individuals. He has something of the explosive vitality of Dickens, much of the concentrated power of making a thing actual which distinguishes Tolstoy, more than a touch of the ethical fervour of Dostoievsky. He has nothing of the amused, even if tender, detachment of a Jane Austen, or the serene aloofness of a Flaubert: there is not an atom of irony in him. Nor is he, it may be repeated, among those moderns who explore, or exploit, a corner of sensibility. His failures, where they occur, are not failures of meagreness, but rather failures to reduce to order a too tumultuous material. As to the realm to which he belongs, he is essentially modern. In his earlier days he was part and parcel of that movement of revolt against accepted social tradition which characterized the pre-war period; and now he is equally modern in trying to make some background, to 'build up new little habitats' he would say, to raise up fresh systems to replace those shattered by the war. Throughout his career he has been anti-materialistic, since materialism for him blunts sensibility, but he is for shearing away the relics of dead faiths or philosophies that clog the free play of the impulses, and he rejects Christianity and Platonism with equal scorn.   He is, in short, anarchic, but anarchic with a formative purpose: he would like to found a new religion.

Since he has here been considered as a writer of prose and not of verse, no examples of the latter have been given. But it may be allowable to quote one of the poems which enter into the novel texture of *The Plumed Serpent*, that strange vision of life and death, containing almost an urgency towards death, such as, in a brilliant essay, he noted in Walt Whitman.   These poems, in their setting, come with something of the grandeur and finality of the choruses in a Greek tragedy.   It is curious to note, in contradistinction with the vividly actual prose of the book, a deliberate, Swinburnian, fugitiveness of imagery.

> The Lord of the Morning Star
> Stood between the day and the night:
> As a bird that lifts its wings, and stands
> With the bright wing on the right
> And the wing of the dark on the left,
> The Drawn Star stood into sight.
>
> Lo!   I am always here!
> Far in the hollow of space
> I brush the wing of the day
> And put light on your face.
> The other wing brushes the dark.
> But I, I am always in place.
>
> Yea, I am always here.   I am Lord
> In every way.   And the lords among men
> See me through the flashing of wings.
> They see me and lose me again.
> But lo! I am always here
> Within ken.
>
> The multitudes see me not.
> They see only the waving of wings,
> The coming and going of things.
> The cold and the hot.

But ye that perceive me between
The tremors of night and the day,
I make you the Lords of the Way
Unseen.

The path between gulfs of the dark and the steeps of the light;
The path like a snake that is gone, like the length of a fuse to ignite
The substance of shadow, that bursts and explodes into sight . . .

I am far beyond
The horizons of love and strife.
Like a star, like a pond
That washes the lords of life.

It is with that echo in your ears that I would like to leave
him with you.

T. S. ELIOT[1]

IN selecting a contemporary poet for my subject, I have been guided by much the same considerations as led me in choosing contemporary novelists. I have ruled out the older modern writers, distinguished as at least three of the late Victorians are, and two of them still actively writing, because they express attitudes towards life which are not of this time. For another reason—frankly because I do not think them of much value, in spite of a deal of charm—I have passed by those who made their name in immediately pre-war days, namely the 'Georgian Poets'; they walk in the path of an older poetic faith; the landscape around them has altered, and they have not noticed the change. I have excluded Mr. Yeats and Mr. De la Mare because they are poets of escape into a fairy world and a dream world,[2] and I wished to hit upon somebody who represents the tangled aspects of our day. Remain the Sitwells, and Mr. Robert Graves. Miss Edith Sitwell appears to me to have developed a technique beyond her thought, to go too far in the direction of poetry meant only for the ear. Mr. Sacheverell Sitwell, a most seductive poet, seems to let too much slip through his fingers, carried away by a very gracious poetic talent which includes a sweetness equal to Marvell's. In fact Mr. Graves, to my mind, is the only

[1] Since this lecture was written, Mr. Eliot has published a book of essays, *For Lancelot Andrewes*, and a poem, *A Song for Simeon*, which considerably clarify his view, and must modify much of what I have said. I have therefore added a postscript to the lecture.

[2] I was not at that time acquainted with Yeats's later work, 1963.

serious competitor.   Both as a poet and a critic he represents our time—and a good poet does profoundly represent
his time, the stress being on the word profoundly.   Mr.
Graves attacks gaily from all sorts of unexpected angles.
But he has, to my thinking, made the wrong choice of two
choices possible at the present day, whereas Mr. Eliot has
made the right one.   The choices I mean concern the background of thought and poetry essential to every age.   The
Greeks had their Pantheon and Fate; Dante St. Thomas and
the whole corpus of scholastic writing; the seventeenth-
century poets were confused, but they had a background of
surging life.   Now, with the collapse of dogmatic Christianity, where is this background to be found? There is no
accepted faith, no agreed politic, or even morality; all is
at sixes and sevens; but there are the two new sciences
which are doing much to alter our outlook upon the world;
the new psychology of Freud, Jung, and such-like, which
Mr. Graves has chosen; and anthropology, especially as
regards the basis of the older religions, which Mr. Eliot has
taken for his province.   That is to say, Mr. Graves breaks
with tradition,[1] Mr. Eliot enters still further into it.

For Mr. Eliot is a traditional poet, not in any bad way
of passive imitation, but in the way which he himself has
taken the trouble to define when speaking of other poets.
That is, he has the historical sense, 'which is', he says, 'a
sense of the timeless and of the temporal together'.   A poet
of tradition is intensely aware of all that has gone before;
he feels that he is adding something to a great structure of
poetry, and that if he adds anything, what he adds will
slightly change the aspect of all that has already been done.
The sense of tradition, Mr. Eliot adds, 'is at the same time
what makes a writer most acutely conscious of his place in
time, his contemporaneity'.

[1] This is no longer true.   See *The White Goddess* and other writings by
Mr. Graves. [1963]

To follow a track discovered and already trodden by Mr. Aldington, we may say that Mr. Eliot is the child of two currents of poetic attitude, streams which always flow, though they may sometimes disappear from the landscape of a period. He is the child on the one hand of the *poète contumace*, tracing his descent through Laforgue, Corbière, and such-like, to Skelton and Villon. The contumacious poet is one who finds himself ill at ease in life, unable to accept current valuations, urged to mock, to flout, to outrage; he is hurt by life; he will harden, but cannot rot into cynicism. Such an attitude is by no means necessarily a shallow one; the disturbance may be very profound, but it can hardly by itself make a great poet, though it may make one who bears much fruit in his successors. There must be another quality, and Villon had such, not easily definable, a largeness of vision Corbière certainly had not. Laforgue had the exquisite wistfulness which often marks the consumptive, a Heine, or a Novalis. Mr. Eliot was at one time easily comparable with Laforgue; not because he imitated him—Mr. Eliot does not imitate—but, though he never exhibited his inherent weaknesses, he had reached much the same mental position as Laforgue. He did not stay there, he could not have stayed there—perhaps Laforgue could not have stayed there had he lived—and then his second line of descent, one through the metaphysical poets back to Dante, made itself felt.

But before proceeding to this latter, let us take one or two instances of Mr. Eliot as the contumacious poet. One characteristic of this order of writers is that they will not be bound by any accepted doctrine of poetry; they insist that they may use whatever material they like, whatever diction. They know that it is no good using the old counters. They are witty poets who shock and startle, not from any desire to do so, but from sheer sincerity. As well as any other poem of Mr. Eliot's, we may take *The Love Song of Alfred J. Prufrock.* It begins in a starkly 'modernist' manner:

> Let us go then, you and I,
> When the evening is spread out against the sky
> Like a patient etherised upon a table;
> Let us go, through certain half-deserted streets
> The muttering retreats
> Of restless nights in one-night cheap hotels
> And sawdust restaurants with oyster-shells. . . .

That is deliberately rasping, at any rate in the images it suggests, but we soon pass to phrases that are more likely to be accepted as 'poetic':

> The yellow fog that rubs its back upon the window-panes,
> The yellow smoke that rubs its muzzle on the window-panes.

and we are at once confident that we are in the presence of an original poet, for we have met the creative metaphor; and metaphor, as Aristotle insisted, is the one thing that cannot be learnt or imitated. Then, as we enter into the poem, a number of changing rhythms begets in us a sense of futility, and we learn that Prufrock is a middle-aged man trying to screw up his courage to propose, but not daring to 'disturb the universe', as he feels, the ordered accustomed sequence of tea-cups, coffee-spoons, and the so-called cultured babble of the drawing-room. In despair Prufrock realizes:

> I should have been a pair of ragged claws
> Scuttling across the floors of silent seas;

an Elizabethan image that, reminiscent of Donne or Webster, surprising, biting, and unforgettable; unforgettable as Donne's

> A bracelet of bright hair about the bone;

or Webster's

> A dead man's skull beneath the roots of flowers,

both of which lines Mr. Eliot himself has quoted on occasion. So the poem goes on, with Prufrock ruefully analysing his indecision, facing his inadequacy. And then, at the very end, in a manner favourite with Mr. Eliot, the particular is suddenly made general, the minute emotion caught up and embodied in a larger sphere, by a violent contrast between the ugly and inane on the one hand, and the beautiful—let us use the cant word—charged with meaning on the other. But they are unified; they are different aspects of the same thing:

> I grow old . . . I grow old. . . .
> I shall wear the bottoms of my trousers rolled.
>
> Shall I part my hair behind? Do I dare to eat a peach?
> I shall wear white flannel trousers, and walk upon the beach.
> I have heard the mermaids singing, each to each.
>
> I do not think that they will sing to me.
>
> I have seen them riding seaward on the waves
> Combing the white hair of the waves blown back
> When the wind blows the water white and black.
>
> We have lingered in the chambers of the sea
> By sea-girls wreathed in seaweed red and brown
> Till human voices wake us, and we drown.

There is no need to draw attention to the poetic mastery of those lines, the subtle rhythms, the play of vowel-sounds, the vividness of the imagery; they may be noted once for all as qualities ever present in Mr. Eliot's poetry.

Before leaving Mr. Eliot as the contumacious poet, there is another side of his work which needs stressing, and that is the quality of wit which he, among others, is re-introducing into English poetry; a quality which connects him with the contumacious poets, such as Baudelaire and Catullus on the one hand, and with the metaphysical poets such as Marvell and Donne on the other.   And by wit I do not mean the light, trivial thing we now usually mean by the word, but almost, as Mr. Eliot himself suggests, what Coleridge meant by imagination, 'the balance or reconcilement of opposite or discordant qualities; of sameness with difference; of the general with the concrete . . . judgement ever awake and steady self-possession, with enthusiasm and feeling profound or vehement'.   Mr. Eliot develops this.   Wit is not erudition, though it belongs to a developed mind.   'It is not cynicism, though it has a kind of toughness which may be confused with cynicism by the tender-minded . . . it implies a constant inspection and criticism of experience. . . . It involves, probably, a recognition implicit in the expression of every experience, of other kinds of experience.'   He sums it up as a 'tough reasonableness'.   To illustrate this side, one might choose the first part of a poem called *Mr. Eliot's Sunday Morning Service*, which he heads with a quotation from Marlowe's *Jew of Malta*: 'Look, look, master, here come two religious caterpillars.'   In this poem he is contrasting, and we shall meet the contrast again with him, the intensity of religious feeling in the past with its dogmatic death now; and the reality, the concentration of thought and emotion in bygone ages with their superficiality at the present day. He begins with an old joke as to the fecundity of parsons, expressed in one portentous word which occupies the whole of the first line:

> Polyphiloprogenitive
> The sapient sutlers of the Lord
> Drift across the window-panes.
> In the beginning was the Word.

In the beginning was the Word
Superfetation of το ἕυ,
And at the mensual turn of time
Produced enervate Origen.

A painter of the Umbrian school
Designed upon a gesso ground
The nimbus of the Baptized God.
The wilderness is cracked and browned.

But through the water pale and thin
Still shine the unoffending feet,
And there above the painter set
The Father and the Paraclete.

It is different in matter and form from Marvell's

The grave 's a fine and private place
But none I think do there embrace;

it is different also from the poem in which Donne makes an
unselective flea serve as an argument for love, but the same
qualities are there; the connexion of apparently dissimilar
things, and the implication of other experiences.

I have been led insensibly into tracing Mr. Eliot's other
line of descent, that from the metaphysical poets, by
accentuating one aspect of the contumacious poet, for it is
one of Mr. Eliot's virtues that he fuses so much. Let us
see him for one moment as a metaphysical poet pure and
simple, one to whom thought is emotion, an experience
modifying the sensibility, as he himself says of Donne; for
he hopes for, indeed in some respects exemplifies, a return
to the seventeenth century, before the dissociation of man
into two parts, mind and sense, set in. The passage is
taken from a second-period poem of remarkable power and
beauty, Gerontion. But first I will quote a morsel from an
Elizabethan dramatist, Chapman, one that Mr. Aldington
has provided for comparison in an essay upon Mr. Eliot, an
essay from which I have already thieved outrageously:

> Oh, of what contraries consists a man!
> Of what impossible mixtures! vice and virtue,
> Corruption and eterness, at one time,
> And in one subject, let together, loose!
> We have not any strength but weakens us.
> No greatness but doth crush us into air.
> Our knowledges do light us but to err,
> Our ornaments are burthens: our delights
> Are our tormentors: fiends that, raised in fears
> At parting shake our roofs about our ears.

Turning to a corresponding passage in Mr. Eliot, we are aware not only of a different rhythm, more complex as our feeling is more complex, but of a deepening, of an accretion of experience, which the centuries between the Elizabethans and ourselves have brought. It has greater nervous sensibility, it is more intimate, yet there is a sense of wider spaciousness; he is not only generalizing about men as individuals, he is expressing the fate of mankind:

> After such knowledge, what forgiveness? Think now
> History has many cunning passages, contrived corridors
> And issues, deceives with whispering ambitions,
> Guides us by vanities. Think now
> She gives when our attention is distracted
> And what she gives, gives with such supple confusions
> That the giving famishes the craving. Gives too late
> What's not believed in, or if still believed,
> The memory only, reconsidered passion. Gives too soon
> Into weak hands, what's thought can be dispensed with
> Till the refusal propagates a fear. Think
> Neither fear nor courage saves us. Unnatural vices
> Are fathered by our heroism. Virtues
> Are forced upon us by our impudent crimes.
> These tears are shaken by the wrath-bearing tree.

With these few quotations in mind, we may turn to Mr. Eliot's own conception of what a poet is, of what he tries to do. Firstly, to begin with a negation, and I place this in the front rank because it disposes of a fallacy too current for some decades, he declares that it is not the business of the poet to express his personality. Impersonality, anonymity, to adopt Mr. Forster's suggestion, is the first recognizable quality in all great art.[1] The personal experience, even, is nothing; either it is common, or it is incomprehensible to others; not until it is detached, has itself become part of the poet's material, can he use it for purposes of art. For he 'is occupied with the struggle—which constitutes life for a poet—to transmute his personal and private agonies into something rich and strange, something universal and impersonal'. His progress is 'a continual self-sacrifice, a continual extinction of his personality'. One might add that the poet, if he has a personality, need not be afraid that it will be denied scope; but it will be as the instrument, and not as the thing made.

Further, no valuable transformations of the poet's feelings can take place unless he can relate them to the knowledge of his day, which includes the knowledge of the past; and by knowledge is not meant scientific knowledge, nor philosophy, nor religion, but rather that mixture of all, combined with emotion and feeling, which makes up attitudes towards life. The poet must primarily be an absorber of knowledge, though he need not be learned. Mr. Eliot develops this by the aid of a scientific analogy. Chemists know that when some two substances are put together, nothing occurs until a third substance, a catalytic agent, is introduced. Then the two first combine to form a new substance, but the agent remains unchanged. The poet is the agent, the new substance is his poetry. 'The poet's mind is in fact a receptacle for seizing and storing up numberless feelings, phrases, images, which remain there until all the particles which can unite to form a new compound are present together.' Like Keats, he would

---

[1] Cf. Meredith's: A song seraphically free
From taint of personality.

have the poet possess 'no identity';   his artist is the 'nominal artist' of Charlotte Brontë.

This, we can see, is far from any semi-ethical vapour-izings; no criterion of mere sublimity cuts any ice. 'For it is not the "greatness", the intensity, of the emotions, the components,' Mr. Eliot declares, 'but the intensity of the artistic process, the pressure, so to speak, under which the fusion takes place, that counts.'

'Not the intensity of the emotions. . . .' What a relief to hear this after the cult of the Whitmanesque 'barbaric yawp'! in the midst of running after sensation, of the doctrine of passion for passion's sake! The pressure of the artistic process is something different from the pressure of the emotions; we meet it, for instance, in *Lear*, or *Wuthering Heights*. And if we ask whether it is present in Mr. Eliot himself, we can find more than a vague degree of it in *Whispers of Immortality*.

> Webster was much possessed by death
> And saw the skull beneath the skin;
> And breastless creatures under ground
> Leaned backwards with a lipless grin.
>
> Daffodil bulbs instead of balls
> Stared from the sockets of the eyes!
> He knew that thought clings round dead limbs
> Tightening its lusts and luxuries.
>
> Donne, I suppose, was such another
> Who found no substitute for sense;
> To seize and clutch and penetrate,
> Expert beyond experience,
>
> He knew the anguish of the marrow
> The ague of the skeleton;
> No contact possible to flesh
> Allayed the fever of the bone. . . .

There is poetic pressure there; one may, if one likes, guess at all sorts of personal emotions behind it, but the poem is a statement, namely (in its entirety), that though the flesh to-day may be opulent

> . . . our lot crawls between dry ribs
> To keep our metaphysics warm.

It is far from the pretentiousness of the romantics, who wrote in an age when the poet hoped to be priest and prophet as well as singer, but it is fiery. The result is excitement in the reader, not active, but allied to a state of contemplation, an especial kind of excitement, that which Coleridge asked for, 'a more than usual state of emotion with more than usual order'. For, one cannot repeat it too often, it is not the business of art just to express the intense emotions; a dog does that when he bays the moon; but to discipline and control them, to bring them into order. The pressure necessary to do this Mr. Eliot exhibits still more strongly in later work, where the image is more incisively used; and the image is (as he reminds us) the object which the poet produces as correlative with his feelings; it is the means by which the feelings are objectified, and freed of the artist's personality.

> We are the hollow men
> We are the stuffed men
> Leaning together
> Headpiece filled with straw.   Alas!
> Our dried voices, when
> We whisper together
> Are quiet and meaningless
> As wind in dry grass
> Or rats' feet over broken glass
> In our dry cellar.

'We are the hollow men, we are the stuffed men'; those lines explain Mr. Eliot's contumaciousness, why he is dissatisfied with his time. There is in our day no order, no hierarchy, in the intellectual or moral worlds. Our

religion, dragging its tattered garments about the globe,
no longer has intellectual authority. Philosophy, such is
Mr. Eliot's view, is corrupted by the time-philosophy
popularized by M. Bergson, vulgarized by Herr Spengler,
prattled in coteries, drawing-rooms, and studios. Everything is supposed to be in flux; the intellectual and moral
worlds are nerveless and pulpy, as it were awaiting a sign.
Our epoch then is devoid of structure, empty of present
hope. A dreary enough view, you may say. Perhaps, but
it is not new; nor is it the whole of Mr. Eliot's view, as
it is that of some of his immediate predecessors. For who
are the great figures—apart from the Poet Laureate,[1] whose
somewhat removed classicism has made him secure of a
place, but barren of influence? There is Hardy, who
exploited the grandeur of pessimism; Mr. Housman with
his chiselled pessimism, telling us that

> . . . when men think they fasten
> Their hands upon their hearts:

there is Mr. Kipling with his philosophy of nihilism, which
cries out for action as the only hope man has of opposing
himself to a great inane. Mr. Eliot exhibits this pessimism,
but differently. He has not lost faith in the possibilities of
man, but he has a deep realization, in common with many
of the more philosophic thinkers of the day, that this is a
desert period. 'This is cactus land, this is dead land.'
And he feels it profoundly, perhaps as a man, but that is
none of our business, certainly as a poet. For since the
poet must needs be of his time, the poet of to-day has no
framework for his poetry, no traditional belief. He is in
the same plight as the novelist. It does not make poetry
impossible—Shakespeare, who lived in an equally untra-
ditional, if richer time, is there to prove it—but it makes
the poet's task infinitely harder, his achievement much

[1] Then Dr. Robert Bridges. [1963]

more uncertain. For besides making poetry, he has to forge his own philosophy, which may be his ruin, as it was the ruin of Blake. For, as Mr. Eliot insists, it is not a poet's business to philosophize; he exists as the fusing medium, the catalytic agent, of the currents of thought and emotion of his day. Thus Mr. Eliot cannot but express the chaos, the sterility, the spiritual bankruptcy of our time. Yet, 'pessimist' as he is, thus far, he does not think the position final; he is not in the same closed box as Hardy, Housman, and Kipling. He believes we are in a transition stage; and this may bring us to what is so far his greatest poetic achievement, *The Waste Land*.

It is not the statement of a philosophy, for, as Mr. Eliot has remarked, a poem should not express a philosophy, it should replace it. The business of a poet is not with precise thought, but with precise emotion, which is not so common as may be supposed, and is itself the result of thought. It is an extremely complex poem. It could not fail to be, if it is, as I believe, the most significant poem of our time; for this is a complex age, and if the poet is to be at all comprehensive, he must bring together a great many disparate elements. 'The ordinary man's experience', Mr. Eliot writes, 'is chaotic, irregular, fragmentary. He falls in love or reads Spinoza, and these experiences have nothing to do with each other, or with the noise of the typewriter or the smell of cooking; in the mind of the poet these experiences are always forming new wholes.' There again Mr. Eliot reveals his desire for unity.

But the greater the complexity, the more need for a scaffolding of tradition, or an informing faith. These lacking, for scaffolding Mr. Eliot has chosen, as I indicated earlier, anthropology; and the particular theme he has taken for this poem is the legend of the Holy Grail as analysed by ethnologists to be a variant of fertility myths. To put it roughly, the Holy Grail is resident in a castle kept

by the Fisher King.   Only when the Grail manifests itself
are the knights of the castle physically and spiritually
nourished, and the waters released to fructify the earth.
Moreover, bound up with fertility rites is the idea of a
cycle, of eternal recurrence.   We are now at the nadir of
existence; this, our own time, is the Waste Land; the
Fisher King has lost his virility.   But because life is cyclic,
this epoch is not final; there will be resuscitation.   The
immediate outlook, nevertheless, is gloomy enough:

> What are the roots that clutch, what branches grow
> Out of this stony rubbish?

This is the main theme which runs through the poem:

> Here is no water but only rock
> Rock and no water and the sandy road. . . .
>
> There is not even silence in the mountains
> But dry sterile thunder without rain. . . .
>
> If there were water
> And no rock
> If there were rock
> And also water
> And water
> A spring
> A pool among the rock
> If there were the sound of water only
> Not the cicada
> And dry grass singing
> But sound of water over a rock
> Where the hermit-thrush sings in the pine trees
> Drip drop drip drop drop drop drop
> But there is no water.

It is an extraordinarily allusive poem, with references to all
sorts of writings, from St. Augustine to Gérard de Nerval,
from Buddha's Fire Sermon, through Ovid and Dante to
Verlaine.   We have Sir James Frazer and *The Golden Bough*;

the Tarot pack of cards. It sounds chaotic enough, yet all
these things are definitely fused; the result is symphonic,
not episodic; it is, I think, the first thing of its kind in
poetry. Much as the scene varies, the personages in this
poem are really one, or rather two, a man and a woman;
the man a Smyrna merchant, a London clerk, a drowned
Phoenician sailor; the woman a fortune teller, a society
woman, a barmaid, Queen Elizabeth, and there are suggestions of Cleopatra; but both are united in the person of
Tiresias, double-sexed. All the while we have the feeling
that the aridity of the present is contrasted with the fullness
of the past. Yet time is abolished; the traditional poet
makes the past as important and living as the present; the
ages are fused together just as soul and sense are made one,
and the sexes are fused in Tiresias. The binding is achieved
largely by certain groups of references strung through the
poem—the dryness, the legend of Philomel, and the
unreality of great cities. Some of it is composed in col-
loquial public-house English; other parts have a gorgeous-
ness which makes Keats himself sound thin, as Miss Riding
and Mr. Graves have shown by an apt comparison in a
recent book. No idea of this poem can be given by
extracts; it must be read in its entirety, for every part is
essential to every other; its effect is cumulative, since the
poem is magnificently built up with dramatic changes of
movement; but I will quote a short passage leading to the
close; for the close, on account of its back-references, is
incomprehensible without having read the earlier parts.
This passage contains many elements of Mr. Eliot's method;
regular verse and free verse; the metaphysical poet and the
contumacious poet: a transformed popular quotation from
Goldsmith; a line out of *The Tempest*, and a superb finale.
One cannot deny the presence of feelings profound and
vehement. It comes after the description of a sordid love
affair between a typist, and

A small house-agent's clerk, with one bold stare,
One of the low on whom assurance sits
As a silk hat on a Bradford millionaire,

while over them hovers Tiresias, murmuring:

I who have sat by Thebes below the wall
And walked among the lowest of the dead.

This is the passage:

She turns and looks a moment in the glass,
Hardly aware of her departed lover;
Her brain allows one half-formed thought to pass:
'Well now that's done: and I'm glad it's over.'
When lovely woman stoops to folly and
Paces about her room again, alone,
She smoothes her hair with automatic hand
And puts a record on the gramophone.

'This music crept by me upon the waters'
And along the Strand, up Queen Victoria Street.
O City city, I can sometimes hear
Beside a public bar in Lower Thames Street,
The pleasant whining of a mandoline
And a clatter and a chatter from within
Where fishmen lounge at noon: where the walls
Of Magnus Martyr hold
Inexplicable splendour of Ionian white and gold.

The range of the poem is immense; Herr Curtius has suggested that it might be taken as a decorated comment on the history of religion. In so far as it is traditional, in the sense that I have defined, following Mr. Eliot, it is such; but it is far more. It is a concentration under terrific poetic pressure of many of the attitudes, impulses, emotions of our day, through which runs a vague but powerful love, or rather sex-theme, the whole overshadowed by the knowledge of death. To try to explain the poem would be fruitless; every good poem is its own only possible explanation. Yet one may point out that it accomplishes a considerable feat, for it succeeds in being a valid, that is, an amazingly satisfying poem, without appealing to any belief, as Mr. Richards has pointed out. He suggests, in short, that Mr. Eliot has achieved the impossible by doing without a background, but this is to neglect certain implications. For, as Mr. Eliot has commented on this, his doubt is itself a sort of belief; and he concludes, 'It takes application, and a kind of genius, to believe anything, and to believe *anything* (I do *not* mean merely to believe in some "religion") will probably become more and more difficult as time goes on.' Mr. Eliot himself is always passionately searching for something to believe in. He has affinity with those who, like him, see with alarm the deliquescence of our age, the sloppy popular time-philosophies, romanticisms, and idealisms, bolstered up by vulgar conceptions of relativity: he can be connected with Mr. Irving Babbitt in America, Herr Curtius in Germany, Messieurs Benda and Maritain in France, though I do not wish to be accused of the critical error of confusing those persons, nor of suggesting that his solution is theirs. Like many, he looks back to St. Thomas, not to share his beliefs, but to seek help from his approach, his psychological method, his theory of cognition. But above all, Mr. Eliot, if I rightly understand his recent utterances, looks to the will to oppose the flux—that new god which might figure side by side with the god Vortex in a comedy by some new Aristophanes. He believes that there is a changeless truth, the search for which is the main object of man's will, and without which man's will would be meaningless.

It is impossible for any one to see his contemporaries clearly. I hope I have not traduced Mr. Eliot in any way: but before concluding, I must face certain objections. First, his allusiveness. I do not deny that this may sometimes be a check to full understanding; it is a pitfall

Mr. Eliot does not always avoid. But it cannot to-day be helped that a poet should be specialized, just as all of us are getting more and more folded into compartments: he must use the 'material' at his disposal. But this does not prevent our enjoying Mr. Eliot's poetry. Secondly, it is said, he is a difficult poet. That is to some extent true, but every good poet is a difficult poet. Indeed, every work of art, if it is really original, if it is a new synthesis, a new exploration of life, must at first repel. If a work is at once easy to understand, if it asks no effort from ourselves, if, so to speak, it melts like butter in the mouth, well, it just melts, and we have nothing left. But if we at first rebel—and from the inborn laziness of human nature we are likely to resent anything which will force us to re-valuation—it means that the work is a live thing. To understand a work of art is to be in some sort changed: it is an important experience. Art is not a gentle soporific, an escape, an ornament: it is a terrifying thing that must be grappled with, overcome, absorbed. But we cannot all at once take in a new work of art, apprehend a new mind; and Mr. Eliot, as though he kept this in view, everywhere offers us a bridge. He gives us much of the old beauty we are accustomed to, phrases that linger in the ear, images that we do not forget. Then little by little we piece together, first a passage, then a poem; then finally, perhaps, *The Waste Land*, though this must be read again and again. Every time it is a fresh poem, every time it stirs us anew. We need not understand all of Mr. Eliot to capture something of the stuff which nourishes, satisfies, and keeps alert.

Nor is Mr. Eliot always 'difficult'. As a last quotation I will give a short recent poem of his, part of a Christmas series, namely *Journey of the Magi*:

'A cold coming we had of it,
Just the worst time of the year
For a journey, and such a long journey:

The ways deep and the weather sharp,
The very dead of winter.' [1]
And the camels galled, sore-footed, refractory,
Lying down in the melting snow.
There were times we regretted
The summer palaces on slopes, the terraces,
And the silken girls bringing sherbet.
Then the camel men cursing and grumbling
And running away, and wanting their liquor and women,
And the night fires going out, and the lack of shelters,
And the cities hostile and the towns unfriendly
And the villages dirty and charging high prices:
A hard time we had of it.
At the end we preferred to travel all night,
Sleeping in snatches,
With the voices singing in our ears, saying
That this was all folly.

After that comes a descriptive passage, not, as with many poets, to relax the tension, but to enrich it. Most of it is in a rigid metre, rare in English, which reminds one of a Latin hexameter; but it is broken up by lines of a different form. It is a marvellously complex arrangement of stressed and unstressed, long and short syllables, with an astonishing variety of vowel sounds. The imagery is piercing:

Then at dawn we came down to a temperate valley,
Wet, below the snow line, smelling of vegetation;
With a running stream and a water-mill beating the darkness,
And three trees on the low sky,
And an old white horse galloped away in the meadow.
Then we came to a tavern with vine leaves over the lintel,
Six hands at an open door dicing for pieces of silver,
And feet kicking the empty wine-skins.
But there was no information, and so we continued
And arrived at evening, not a moment too soon
Finding the place; it was (you may say) satisfactory.

[1] As a good example of poetic transformation, the reader may be interested to see an extract from a sermon by Lancelot Andrewes, which Mr. Eliot gives in his book dedicated to the bishop. 'It was no summer progress. A cold coming they had of it at this time of the year, just the worst time of the year to take a long journey in. The way deep, the weather sharp, the days short, the sun farthest off, *in solstitio brumali*, the very dead of winter.'

The conclusion contains a variant of the thought in *The Waste Land*. The speaker regrets the loss of the old tradition, the old sureties: the new revelation has dispossessed him of life. Like Mr. Eliot, like the Sybil whom he quotes, he longs for the death that must precede new life, but hating the death which must be the price of new life:

All this was a long time ago, I remember,
And I would do it again, but set down
This set down
This: were we led all that way for
Birth or Death?   There was a Birth, certainly,
We had evidence and no doubt.   I had seen birth and death,
But had thought they were different; this Birth was
Hard and bitter agony for us, like Death, our death.
We returned to our places, these Kingdoms,
But no longer at ease here, in the old dispensation,
With an alien people clutching their gods.
I should be glad of another death.

If that poem needs justification, it is this: it expresses in less than two pages what could not have been expressed in prose, except perhaps in a tedious twenty.   It is, I believe, classical, that is to say enduring, because it scorns any cheap-jack appeal, any meretricious, so-called 'poetic' adornment.

To conclude, I would say this about Mr. Eliot's work. Though it is impossible for us to see a contemporary plain and see him whole, I am of the opinion that his criticism, with its depth, its wide grasp, its beautiful distinctions, its enthusiasm, and its justice, is the most important in English since Coleridge wrote his *Biographia Literaria*: I am not forgetting Landor and Arnold.   As to his poetry, just as no critic can afford to neglect it now, I am sure that no critic of future ages speaking of this age will be able to give it anything but a preponderating place: and I would be prepared to lay odds that the year 1922, which saw *The Waste Land*, will prove to be as important a year in the history of the development of English poetry as the year 1798, in which Wordsworth and Coleridge produced their transforming volume, *Lyrical Ballads*.

POSTSCRIPT

In *For Lancelot Andrewes* (1928), Mr. Eliot has declared that his 'general point of view may be described as classicist in literature, royalist in politics, and anglo-catholic in religion'. He has not altered his views as to the temper of our time, but he has decided that a cure for its ills lies in a return to order, as implied in the words classicism, toryism, anglo-catholicism—so long as toryism does not mean 'temperate conservatism'. 'Set in order', he prays, 'the things which are wanting among us, and strengthen those which remain and are ready to die.' A critic in *The Times* has found it matter for wonder that the author of *The Waste Land* should come to this position; yet the development conforms to the logic of human emotions. 'Scepticism and disillusion are a useful equipment for religious understanding,' Mr. Eliot now writes in an essay on F. H. Bradley; and to show how he arrives at this may be illustrated by a quotation from his essay on Machiavelli:

Machiavelli was no fanatic; he merely told the truth about humanity. The world of human motives which he depicts is true—that is to say, it is humanity without the addition of super-human Grace. It is therefore tolerable only to persons who have also a definite religious belief; to the effort of the last three centuries to supply religious belief by belief in Humanity the creed of Machiavelli is insupportable. Lord Morley voices the usual modern hostile admiration of Machiavelli when he intimates that Machiavelli saw very clearly what he did see, but that he saw only half of the truth about human nature. What Machiavelli did not see about human nature is the myth of human goodness which for liberal thought replaces the belief in Divine Grace.

Mr. Eliot, then, would sharply oppose humanism and religion, and this point of view he develops in his chapter on Mr. Irving Babbitt. Humanism, as he sees it, is sporadic; it exists momentarily after centuries of religious discipline; it may serve for an individual, but not for a people. 'Humanism is, I think, merely the state of mind of a few persons in a few places at a few times. To exist at all, it is dependent upon some attitude, for it is essentially critical—I would even say parasitical.' It cannot provide the 'inner control'.

He desires order above all things; but people will not submit to order unless they have some end in view. For Mr. Eliot, that end is civilization, 'spiritual and intellectual co-ordination on a high level,' and he does not believe that any force except religion (which implies a church) can conduce to that end. Whether he is right only time can show; and unless mankind submits to some discipline or other, time may not show even that much. Again, whether Mr. Eliot's return [1] to Christianity heralds a general return among intellectuals is, I may repeat, doubtful. It is possible that for purposes of art it might be a good thing for writers to return, since without assumptions art is almost impossible, and to-day even scepticism is meaningless. And if the world is to have order, it must have some symbol for order outside its own immediate concerns. And since Mr. Eliot holds this, he could not be a protestant; his whole theory of poetry as a renunciation of individuality goes to prove it. His is the attitude of Andrewes rather than that of Donne. 'Andrewes's emotion is purely contemplative; it is not personal; it is wholly evoked by the object of contemplation, to which it is adequate.' Donne, on the other hand, 'is continually

---

[1] I say 'return' without being in a position to say whether Mr. Eliot ever departed from it. All I can say is, that his earlier work, if not directly counter to Christianity, shows no dependence upon it.

finding an object which shall be adequate to his feelings.'
Mr. Eliot does not confuse himself with the symbol; he
does not attempt to make himself part of the thing to which
he does homage, and this cuts him off sharply from our
mystico-religious enthusiasts. This is his attitude towards
poetry also.

How far Mr. Eliot's return may influence his poetry it
is too early to say: his latest work shows a difference in
direction, but no loss of power. At least he is relieved of
the necessity for creating his own background, hacking out
his own assumptions, or creating out of the void, trying to
do without any assumptions whatever. It might affect his
art in that it would remove the trouble which irritated the
artist in him to action, and if so his gain would be our loss.
For the ethical writer, should Mr. Eliot exchange the poet
in him for the philosopher, can never, however compelling
he may be, command so wide, nor ultimately so good a
public, as the poet who retains something of his private
uneasiness.

ON TWO PLAYS BY ELIOT

'It is not enough to understand what we ought to be, unless we know what we are; and we do not understand what we are, unless we know what we ought to be.' T. S. Eliot, *'Religion and Literature'*

THE CONFIDENTIAL CLERK

WHATEVER the first reactions to Mr. T. S. Eliot's new play may be, one thing can be claimed for it: it is profoundly original. Not so much in idea, for as Goethe said, it is impossible for anyone to have a thought that has not struck somebody before; all that a man can hope for is to arrive at such by the motions of his own mind. The originality lies in what has been done with the form. Not that there is anything new in the way the piece has been built up; it conforms to the well-tried laws of Sardoodle-dom—the exposition, the *scène à faire*, and so on. The play is original because of the level of existence this kind of play is made to maintain, for the idea has been presented through an improbable medium: Mr. Eliot has made a serious thing out of a farce. Or, from another angle, the originality of the play consists in its being a drastic pushing forward of the old critical comedy which, by making us laugh at and criticize our neighbours, aimed at making us see ourselves as others see us. In this play Mr. Eliot calls upon a higher tribunal by demanding that we see ourselves as our conscience sees us. And what is further original, is his making us accept as the person who is justified the individual who in critical comedy would be the butt. In the old way of writing, the young 'hero' of this play would be the person to be laughed at: he is not fitting into society, it would be said; he is being presumptuous, he is guilty of excess, he thinks about himself too much, he is, possibly, a bit of a prig. But here he is the one character who has solved the problem of how to live. It is as though the self-flagellant, or Alceste, or Sir Positive At-All, were to be the model, not the laughing-stock. The old form has been made to serve a new purpose, and if this is still moralistic, it is so with a difference. Mr. Eliot has not torn the trappings from society; he has not given us a fleeting vision of the terror or the glory of existence; those things are, rather, the province of tragedy. But he has made a rent in the curtain of complacent assumptions, and whether or not his conclusions seem valid, he has at least provided something which in its context is new, and which the imaginative reason can work upon.

The play is a West End success, which means that Mr. Eliot has achieved something without which any other attainment is barren; he is daily capturing the ear and the attention of a large number of people. Whether what he wants to say will penetrate to the majority of his audience is another question, for it may be that he has made the bait so large that the fish can feed lavishly on it without swallowing the hook. To the attentive, it goes without saying, there all the time exists another play at a deeper level than the obvious one, perhaps a third at a level deeper still. But as an amusing comedy erected on a basically farcical situation, opening in such a way as to induce at once that willing suspension of disbelief for the moment which enjoyment demands, it holds from the start. Causing a good deal of laughter by incidental remarks, keeping expectation at full height all the while, and interspersing the action with quiet, rather sad moments (thus relating the play to a comedy of Molière), it amounts, apart from anything else, to a piece of theatrical virtuosity which should ensure it a long run.

It may be as well in the first instance to consider what Mr. Eliot has done to gain popularity, how he has done it, and what price he has had to pay. He has achieved his result by making people laugh: well and good. But, the question arises, What kind of laughter is it, and does it subserve or interfere with the penetrating power of the theme? The laughter he produces is hardly that of wit in the best sense, which appeals to the intellect; nor does it arouse the 'thunders of laughter clearing air and heart', which comes from the realization of the antinomies in man's nature, the absurd contradiction of his being an angel housed in the body of a timid or lustful or cruel beast; it is not great, or ritual laughter. In fact his situations and his remarks are what everybody finds 'funny'; they pro-duce easy chuckles, or even giggles, never on so low a plane that one need be ashamed of them, but of the sort with which lesser popular playwrights lard their plays. This laughter doesn't plunge you deeper, it doesn't open the doors of enlightenment, it doesn't release into a free realm. Though it must be granted that some sort of flavouring must be applied as a sauce to the meat of the serious theme to make it resemble the kind of pabulum the after-dinner playgoer will swallow, it must be recognized that Mr. Eliot takes a tremendous risk in employing this particular one. Maybe it breaks down resistances; but does it make the meaning more transparent? Or does it obscure it? The danger is that more men and women than need be will remain on the surface level of the play, good, flimsy, easily digested entertainment. For some the serious element of the play is so enthralling, that they may find themselves resisting the laughter, brushing away the jokes as if they were bothersome flies; for the jokes tend to distract, to take away the attention from something which really concerns the auditor. This is the main possible blemish of the play, but on the whole it survives it. Mr. Eliot has got a public, though it may not be quite the public that he wants.

It should be said at this point that this review is based upon only seeing the play, which has not been published at the time of writing; there has been no opportunity to ponder the work, to cast back and forth, to realize the implications, ironic or otherwise, that earlier scenes or remarks cast upon later developments, nor to turn over at leisure what it is that Mr. Eliot is fundamentally saying. Reading and re-reading the play will no doubt alter judgment in many respects, and bring out points too easily submerged in the rapidity of the action; for there are, as is manifest in merely hearing the play, a good many passages which will cry out to be lingered over, and of which the significance can seep in only gradually. Nevertheless there is something to be said for considering the first impact of a play seen before being read. After all, a play's a play, not a document to be fumbled. We ask ourselves what mood or temper has been created in the theatre, what 'attitude' induced? Do we wish to brood apart, as after a tragedy? Or does the play, after the manner of comedy, seem 'to make life spin along more briskly'? The answer here is uncertain, for *The Confidential Clerk* would seem to induce a vacillating mood. Something has happened to one, but what exactly? That is no adverse criticism; it is, after all, the first effect of *Measure for Measure*. Perhaps the play is a tragi-comedy. Something good has been destroyed by something lesser or accidental, but a fair proportion of good seems to settle down at the conclusion. All's as well as can be hoped for in a play that ends not too disastrously.

So to try to assess what is the reason for the uncertainty of response, it seems easiest to go back to first principles. Thus granting that any work of art is giving form to the

10

formless, we proceed to ask what in a play is the material
to which form is being given? Is it the bustling, multi-
farious, passionate life all around us, filled with all sorts of
people, unexpected, contradictory, self-denying, cruel and
generous, from whose confused actions some meaning
emerges, some pattern which enlightens life or deepens
apprehension? Or is it an idea, intuition, or religious
gleam or certainty, or some moral conclusion, for which
the characters of the play and their directed actions provide
the symbols? In the first case, which Shakespeare, generally
speaking, exemplifies (*pace* certain modern critics), creation springs from an abundant love of the human creature
as he is, a glorying in the staggering pageant of human
existence. The pattern develops organically, the 'meaning'
oozes as doth the gum from whence 'tis nourished. In the
second, which we meet with on the whole in serious
comedy—think of Molière or Congreve—creation seems
rather to be born from the desire to illustrate the already
conceived pattern; the characters do not exist in life;
they are made as symbols to fit the preconceived moral.
Mr. Eliot, as far as can be judged, works in this latter way.
The difficulty with this creative approach is to keep the
simulated life coherent, to impose upon members of the
audience the level at which they are to exist while watching
the play. In *The Cocktail Party* Mr. Eliot was not altogether
successful so far as this goes; the Guardians were too
puzzling, existing in a dual character; the religious and the
mundane clashed rather than mingled, so that the audience
could never be sure from one moment to another with
what part of themselves they were being asked to apprehend people or events. In the present play there is no such
uneasiness; it is all of a piece, and no sudden reorganiza-
tions of approach are demanded. The people, though they
vary among and in themselves, can all be grasped on the
level of the world we normally inhabit. The skill resides

in having made them at least temporarily plausible, although the story itself is so fantastically and so delightfully improbable.

The persons of the play (which bears, if Mr. Eliot likes, some relation to the *Ion* of Euripides) are Sir Claude Mulhammer, who has an illegitimate son, Colby Simpkins, and an illegitimate daughter, Lucasta Angel. His wife, Lady Elizabeth, also has an illegitimate son, whom she has lost sight of since infancy. B. Khagan, a business man, is a foundling. Eggerson, the retired confidential clerk, to be replaced by Colby, provides the linking element of the play; and Mrs. Guzzard, who appears at the end, rather as a *dea ex machina*, is a foster-mother who unravels the tangles. It is, in short, a farce of mistaken or dubious identity. All that, of course, is only the framework through which the theme has to be revealed. This, as it was put by the B.B.C. 'Critics on the Air', is something like: 'Unless you know who your father is, you don't know who you are: and if you don't know who you are you don't know what you are.' Here is a possible religious significance, if you care to take the play on the third level. The main theme, however, the 'second level' theme, might be what it was in *The Cocktail Party*, namely 'Be the thing you are'—a Shakespearian theme this too. But whereas in the earlier play it came as an injunction, as when Reilly tells Chamberlayne, 'Be content to be the fool you are,' and Celia has to be led to discover herself to be of the stuff of martyrs, in the new play the characters discover for themselves how important it is to find out what they are, and to pursue the appropriate life regardless of conventional standards, and against the pressure of circumstance. Or it might be a development of: 'Until you rid yourself of your fantasies, you will never lead a satisfactory life,' the difference being that here we have a process offered us, rather than a fact we have to accept.

In the first act we learn that Mulhammer, now a highly successful financier, had really hankered after being a potter. But realizing that he would never be more than a second-rate craftsman, he took the opportunity of going into finance, to which he cannot wholly give himself. He remedies his frustration by collecting pottery, and withdrawing from time to time into the refuge of his collection, where, though not 'transfigured by the vision of some marvellous creation', he can escape from the unreality of his business life. It is, he admits, a kind of make-believe, but the belief makes it real; he supposes his devotion to ceramics takes the place of religion. (We all know what Mr. Eliot thinks of that kind of substitute.) The theme will recur again; but in this act Mulhammer opens up a second one, that of continuity, not so much of heredity, as it seemed to the critic of *The Times*, but of tradition symbolized by paternity. His father had left him the business, and the son had wished (all this is a little vague, and would need reading to clarify) to fulfil himself in what his father had wished to fulfil. The words 'reconcilement' and 'atonement' occur, perhaps—the suggestion is a little in the air—for the sins of the father, such as Lord Monchesney in *The Family Reunion* had felt the urgency of. All this comes out because the young man himself would like to be a musician. Both know, however, that Colby would be only a second-rate musician, so Sir Claude comforts his son by expatiating on the value of his own solution. To give Colby the same comfort he will set him up in a nice flat with a first-rate piano, so that he also can escape from the hollowness of business into the realm he would wish to inhabit.

The second act, which takes place in Colby's flat, develops the theme of the double life in the course of a touching scene portraying an incipient love affair between Colby and Lucasta, each ignorant of the other's parentage.

Colby, luxuriating in receptive sympathy, describes how his musical life is like a garden to him, into which he can withdraw, locking the gates behind him. A little sentimental, perhaps, but after all, second-rate artists often are sentimental. Thus the theme of loneliness is introduced, a loneliness which can be broken down only by the continual and progressive understanding of others. Somebody must join him in his garden, but he cannot invite anybody; he or she must somehow come in gradually of their own wish. He is groping after some reconciliation with being —really a religious impulse; for though he tells Lucasta (from prison?) that he is not religious, she quite rightly tells him that she thinks he is; and when he speaks of the companion in the garden, there is a faint suggestion that he is Adam, hoping not only for an Eve-Lucasta, but remembering that 'Adam in the garden walked with God'. That level, however, is glanced at rather than reached, and we are stood firmly on the second level with a gloss on Mulhammer's thesis, namely that if you lead two lives which have no connection with each other, neither of them is real. On the ostensible level, that of comedy, the love-affair is developing well, until Lucasta tells Colby that she is Mulhammer's daughter. This provides the most dramatic, and emotionally deepest moment of the play. Colby recoils from her as a lover at the revelation that she is his half-sister, but is unable to tell her what the revulsion is due to, since he has promised not to reveal the secret of his parentage: she is thrown into despair, believing that his evident horror is on account of her being a bastard. Finding herself thus permanently outcast, she is prepared to link herself with the vulgar, breezy, eupeptic Khagan, who opportunely appears; being a quite happy foundling he doesn't see that it matters in the least who your father is. Enter then Lady Elizabeth, and soon afterwards Mulhammer, and we revert to the sheer imbroglio of farce, enormously entertaining on a very light level. Husband and wife each claim Colby as their son; and to disentangle the matter, it is decided to call in the Mrs. Guzzard who fostered the young man, and who, by a freak of chance, will also provide a clue as to where Lady Elizabeth's son may be found if he is not Colby. Eggerson, who is intimately acquainted with Sir Claude's affairs, will be summoned to act as chairman of the meeting.

The last act resolves the two themes, the resolution bringing as corollaries a good number of philosophico-religious considerations, such as the virtue of obedience to facts, the equal virtue of knowing the limits of one's understanding of other people, the having to adapt one's self to the granting of one's wishes. In the event, Lady Elizabeth's son turns out to be Khagan, a fact neither of them recognizes with rapturous enthusiasm; while as to Sir Claude, Mrs. Guzzard shatters him with the fact that his son had never been born, Colby being her own by her long deceased husband who was a second-rate organist. She can supply substantial evidence. Colby is delighted. He can drop the silly business of being confidential clerk to a financier, and pass his life as a second-rate organist; and, as is proper to farce, he is at once offered a post by Eggerson. Lucasta is going to marry Khagan, so she fades out of Colby's picture, apparently unregretted. And here perhaps is the main dramatic weakness of the play: expectation has been aroused by the moving Colby-Lucasta scene in the second act, but the theme drops lifeless from Eliot's hand. The young man, regardless of earlier passages, with immense satisfaction declares: 'Now that I know who my father is, I can follow him.' But Sir Claude is broken (though Lucasta tries to comfort him); the cherished hope of having a son to follow him is shattered; further, Lady Elizabeth tells him she would far rather have had him for a husband as a second-rate potter than as an important financier who, she fancied, had married her only because he wanted a hostess. There we touch the element of tragedy, the something good that is broken.

And now we ask, where has Mr. Eliot got to in his fascinating journey as a playwright? What has he accomplished? What appalling difficulties has he overcome? For he is not a playwright by nature; the stage was not originally his chosen medium, and his great triumph consists in having made himself into a dramatist whose work the great multitude of playgoers will accept and enjoy. But what were the problems apart from that *sine qua non* which he had to tackle?

For one, there was that of embedding in the play itself the memorable utterances, the *sententiae*, which every great or even good play must carry. In his earlier plays, Mr. Eliot, in common with other of his contemporaries, went back to the device of the chorus; forthrightly in *Murder in the Cathedral*; with an ingenious modification in *The Family Reunion*, where the characters occasionally group themselves as chorus; and with almost complete camouflage in *The Cocktail Party*, where only the big 'libation' scene is an obvious reminder. He has now completely rid himself of this device; he gets his general statements uttered by the characters as such; and if the 'moral sentences' seem to crowd in rather thick and fast in the last act, the characters can sustain them in the speed and excitement of the action. For example, there is the comparison of Eggerson's 'escape' with that of Colby. Colby's garden—at least as far as others are told about it—is simply a place to go into, a haven in which to indulge the self-regarding virtues. Eggerson, in his outer suburb, has a plot of ground into which he escapes from the little irritations of daily living, the household chores, the domestic adjustments, wanting simply to be with himself. The stated difference is this: nothing comes out of Colby's garden, while Eggerson occasionally brings back from his solitude pumpkins and beans for his wife. The moral is plain, it is humorous, and it comes across charmingly.

Which leads to the question of character. A play is itself a symbol, and whether the pattern emerges from the surge of life or is itself the basis, the characters have to give actuality to the symbol, express it in terms of living. They must achieve verisimilitude, seem to be common flesh and blood, or if uncommon, appear to possess at least nerve and sinew. The danger with Mr. Eliot, who begins with the idea, and mines for the 'objective correlative', is that the characters may obstinately remain vehicles of an idea rather than have a life of their own, as was too much felt in *The Cocktail Party*, not only with the Guardians. And the difficulty he encountered in his new play was to give 'reality' to farcical characters so as to make them more than such, in fact to write a farce with the texture of comedy. For the people in comedy are 'real'—Portia, Célimène, Millamant, Sir Toby, Orgon, Tanner—whereas Charley's Aunt or the people in *The Importance of Being Earnest* are not. Ben Jonson was faced with the same difficulty, which he resolved triumphantly by making his characters from Mosca to Abel Drugger almost desperately concerned with the immediate actualities of life as it has to be lived from day to day, with its complex of duties ('three parts of life'), its idealisms, its lusts, its laziness, its ambitions, sacrifices, and disastrous failures: his are people first and symbols afterwards. Mr. Eliot's beings are not altogether reassuring. One accepts them at the outset in the eager curiosity that possesses the happy playgoer; but as the play goes on the interest shifts from them as fellow-creatures, to the eagerness of seeing how the tangle is going to work out. This perhaps is because they do not solve their problems; their problems are solved for them. Or perhaps it is that Mr. Eliot does not seem to love his people; and to make his people convincing the dramatist must either love them, however little he may think of them, as (since *Measure for Measure* has been instanced) Shakespeare loved Pompey; or sympathise with them so deeply that even his revulsion has a quality of love in it, as with Shakespeare and Angelo. And because none of the people who carry the main themes is lovable the idea is a little weakened, and therefore—since 'the life of comedy is in the idea'—the play itself. Some of the characters we greet as knowable—Sir Claude, Colby, Lucasta; with them we can to some extent experience empathy, though we come away with a little grain of doubt. Are people in truth and experience like that? Sir Claude could possibly live as he does. But are the young people actually young people of to-day, with similar perplexities? They neither get far enough in their love-affair to let us know, nor are they the eternal maid and her wight. So they don't ring quite true as whole human beings; they don't enter into the imagination and seize upon it; we have to make an effort of the imagination to seize them. And when at the end of the play Colby says that what is needed is more love—a phrase which at any rate to-day needs tremendous pressure behind it to make it mean anything (as Yeats said, 'Things thought too long cannot be thought at all')—it carries no conviction whatever, either as a moral sentence or as part of his character. He at any rate shows little sign of being capable of deep affection. There is indeed little sentiment of love anywhere in the play. Mr. Eliot may love his characters, but if so it is in spite of their faults, and not (as with Mirabel and Millamant) because of them. If the play were just a farce and no more this would not matter: but since it is a great deal more, it does in the end count.

A curious point is that on the whole the most lovable person is Eggerson, who is really little more than a stock character, though as such an effective vehicle for that sly genial humour in which Mr. Eliot has never been lacking. He is beautifully 'done', but belongs to the theatre rather than to life; he is brother to the elder Boon in *You Never Can Tell*, the completely understanding old fellow without ambition for himself, wanting to see everybody happy, the *homme de bonne volonté*. Lady Elizabeth is a little ambiguous; she is, if not sister, at least cousin to Julia in *The Cocktail Party*, the difference being that though she lives on two planes of 'reality', she does so unconsciously. Absurdly amusing figure of farce as she is, she nevertheless contributes to the theme as one who tried to break away from family tradition. She even at one time embraced Buddhism, since that religion allowed her to look upon herself as a self-existent soul seeking reincarnation through indifferent parents, mere conveyers, without influence on the essential self. But regarded as an example of Mr. Eliot's technique, she is very much worth attention. This apparently irresponsible, idiotic-fashionable-'intellectual', always hunting after strange gods, can yet be the vehicle of possibly profound utterances—as the divine simpleton of a very complex kind! She is, however, so ambivalent that when she declares 'I don't believe in facts' we do not know whether the remark is profoundly significant, as it might be, or merely silly. Lucasta also is a little indeterminate. Self-protectively flippant, but with a potential depth of which we catch a glimpse in the second act, she lives in a kind of despair at not knowing what she is, hardening herself against frustration by going about as The Girl Who is Always Hungry—a joke which does not really bear the repetition accorded it. So though Mr. Eliot is, we can think, more successful than ever before in giving his characters validity on a definite level, he has not yet quite solved that problem. It is here, possibly, that we find the key to the indeterminate effect of the play.

Where, however, he has achieved complete and triumphant success, is in the matter of stage speech. He has at last among writers of poetic drama broken away from the notion that dramatic blank verse is the iambic pentameter, a silly pedantry that has bedevilled both discussion and practice for a drearily long period. Since the first two lines of *Gorboduc*, dramatic blank verse has never been the iambic pentameter, a most inappropriate measure for the stage, for what the dramatist has to do is to give the actor phrases which he can utter louder than in normal speech —since he has to fill a theatre with sound—and which will bring the stress on the right word. It is no use telling him to let the words come trippingly from the tongue unless you give him words that *can* come trippingly from the tongue. The form which tells best in English is a phrase with normally three stresses, going easily to four and on occasion to five; and whether the phrases are chopped off in sausage-lengths of ten syllables or not, doesn't in the least matter. The advantage of this metre is that it is enormously flexible, and can, when required, reflect the tension of poetry proper, create the ethos in which it can flourish.[1] What Mr. Eliot has done, rather laboriously (as he explains in his extremely interesting *Poetry and Drama*), is to go back to Shakespearian usage, that is, a three-stress line, though he postulates a caesura somewhere, which the Shakespearians didn't care a fig about. What it amounts to is an irregularly anapaestic line, or rather, phrase, for it is of no importance where you end it in print. Take a line or two from *The Cocktail Party* (the text of the present play not being available) choosing practically at random:

> That was a nearer guess than you think.   (3 stress dactylic)
> But permit me to remark that my revelations (4 stress anapaestic)

And now, since *Measure for Measure* has been mentioned,

[1] There is no space to discuss this here. I might perhaps refer any reader who is interested to my *Histriophone*. Hogarth Pamphlets. First Series. 1925.

from that play, where, indeed, Shakespeare uses mainly a four-stress line such as

> Stand like the forfeits in a barber's shop. (V, i)

But take:

> 'Tis one thing to be tempted, Escalus,
> Another thing to fall. I not deny. . . . (II, i)
>   (Both 3 stress, vaguely anapaestic)

or

> Intends you for his swift ambassador (III, i)   (3 stress irregular)

When special emphasis is needed there is the three-stress iambic *phrase* (not line)

> A pond as deep as hell. (III, i)

So Mr. Eliot in the present play:

> And lock the gates behind you,

or Shakespeare in *The Tempest*:

> And makes my labours pleasures. (III, i)

(It must be duly noted that, as Omond said, counting of stresses is only a shade less mechanical than the counting of syllables.)

The result is beautiful stage speech, neither strict nor impeccable prose, but the best possible stage instrument. It is delightful to listen to. Mr. Eliot's sounds like ordinary speech, though it is not so; and I venture to say that in *The Confidential Clerk* we have the most perfect theatre measure since Congreve. This sort of verse can do anything: it can allow Mr. Eliot to write the lovely swinging phrase already quoted—I do not know how he may print it, nor do I greatly care—

> Transfigured by/The vision of some marvellous creation

(How does this differ from 'Swell with the touches of those flower-soft hands'?) and the audience does not notice it at all as special language. The speeches of Sir Claude and Colby in the first act would not come with the trenchancy they do unless they were 'poetry' in this sense; but for the average listener this will be just talk, not verse, which is precisely what Mr. Eliot wants. To the literary detective, whose ear listens delightedly for cadences, what is happening is clear. The verse doesn't in any way interfere, but it has its effect on the audience without their knowing it. Here, then, is perfect mastery. To have swept away the clogging lumber of two centuries itself constitutes an originality. It amounts to the invention of a new verse form, which, as Mr. Eliot himself has remarked in another connection, is the most important thing that can happen to a nation.

These are the elements as they appear from seeing and hearing the play admirably performed. What of the final result?

What exactly, we ask first, was Mr. Eliot trying to do? It's not so easy to say. He is certainly not 'imitating life' so that his audience may catch the glamour and the glory of it. He is not presenting a vision of what life might be to some people, as he was in *Murder in the Cathedral*, and to a lesser degree with Celia in *The Cocktail Party*. He offers a comedy (disguised as farce); and comedy is for those who think, tragedy for those who feel (the old cliché will serve well enough here). He is trying, in short, to make his audience think. But here another seeming anomaly, or originality, crops up. Comedy deals with the relation of people to each other in society, or with their place in society, with their interactions in a social milieu: tragedy deals with the relation of man to God—or whatever name he may be called by. Yet when Colby at the end says 'Now that I know who my father is, I can follow him,' the

subtler implication is, as the B.B.C. Critics suggested, that
we cannot know what we are until we recognize our Father
in Heaven. When earlier he says he wishes he could have
a father who died before him, whom he could reconstruct
from relics and stories, so that he might perhaps live the
life his father would have wished to live, it occurs to some
that what Mr. Eliot means is that we should model ourselves, as far as is humanly possible, upon Christ. Thus
Mr. Eliot's play is really (at the third level, admittedly) a
play dealing with man's relation to God, which would
seem to demand tragic form.

In any event the play, on the second level, is a didactic
play (in a sense, of course, every good play is such), and
Mr. Eliot once again reveals himself as the outstanding
English moralist of our time, at any rate in the literary
sphere. But whereas the moral of comedy is usually 'Fit
yourself into society', here it is 'Follow the indication that
God has given you of the sort of life you ought to lead, the
sort of person you ought to be'. It is, in fact, as some have
called it, 'a religious farce'. Put in another way, however,
the moral is the Delphic adjuration 'Know thyself!', the
Stoic 'Be the thing that you are!' It is, one might feel,
making religion a matter of morality tinged with emotion,
however stoutly Mr. Eliot might repudiate any connection
with Arnold. So now, of course, the question forces itself
upon one as to how far he may be attacking the assumptions
of our day, for this play is, obviously, a criticism of life.
And here our questionings become active. Is it really
better for a man to be a second-rate artist or craftsman than
a thoroughly efficient financier or confidential clerk?
Which best serves society, that is, the individual's fellow
human beings; that is to say, God? Isn't the attitude we
are asked to adopt rather that of those who are the prey of
a self-regarding virtue? Are we to follow our desires as
admittedly second-raters rather than fit into the larger

pattern which the process of society invites us to fill because we are capable of filling it? As Arnold wrote to his mother, 'we are not here to have facilities found for us for doing the work we like, but to make them.' Ought we not to accept the position we find ourselves in, take up our responsibility to society rather than to our very noble selves? After all, as Marcus Aurelius said, 'Even in a palace, life can be led well,' so why not in a City financier's West End mansion? On the other hand the play, the moral, may be a protest against the totalitarian forcing of the social atom to sacrifice his individuality to that nebulous concept 'the general good'. But one must beware of reading more into the play than Mr. Eliot intended; for though he himself has declared that the poet often says more than he knows, to extract what one likes out of any work is surely to miss its vivifying point. But accepting this possible stricture on our civilization, we can still ask whether, if we insist on being second-rate organists rather than good confidential clerks, we are not being guilty of spiritual pride? For humility is the greatest of all traps; a man may find with Benjamin Franklin, who hoped to become humble, that he is proud of his own humility. Yet it may be that Mr. Eliot was following an impulse that has been his from the beginning, at all events since *Prufrock*, and was here criticizing modern civilization on account of the directionless people it produces, and its disruptive, fragmented nature. After all, this play is by the author of *Notes Towards a Definition of Culture* and *After Strange Gods*. But this last idea, if it was intended, is tenuous and not, one supposes, the main theme, though it may be there as an envelope.

So that if now we ask how far Mr. Eliot has succeeded in doing what he wanted to do (besides providing an evening's first-rate entertainment, which he has done), the answer must be uncertain. One has once more to ask the

question: 'What did I feel on coming out of the theatre?
What do I feel—or think—after pondering its impress upon
me? Has anything happened to me? Have I had an
experience?' It is best to put it in this way to avoid the
categorizing habit it is so easy to fall into; present critical
fashion tends to forget that a work of art is unique, every
time raising the naively fundamental questions. Subjective? Yes, of course. All talk of 'concrete standards'
is arid nonsense. Anyone has to ask in the first instance
'What has this work done to me?'—assuming naturally that
the 'I' is a fairly normal person. Then if he likes he can
relate this experience to others, and with some justification
docket and pigeon-hole. And I suppose, judging from
myself, that Mr. Eliot's intention was to make each
member of the audience ask himself 'Am I leading the sort
of life I really ought to be leading? Am I not worshipping
false gods, and whoring after all manner of inventions?'
It is, of course, a salutary question, a question which a man
should from time to time ask that particular priest of
comedy called Common Sense. If this, as I believe, was the
state of mind into which Mr. Eliot wished to throw his
hearers, then he has been successful. If he wished to
persuade us to any sort of doctrine, then, I think, he has
failed. We are told to be obedient to facts, in short, to
accept; but which of us knows what part of ourselves we
ought to accept? and to suppose that we are one kind of
thing only is in contradiction with Mr. Eliot's own at least
partial acceptance of the idea of the fluid personality. We
are all of us a great many things; circumstance perhaps has
made us one thing rather than another. Of course to
swallow the obvious stated moral *au pied de la lettre* would
be sheer nonsense. We don't for our salvation necessarily
have to follow in father's footsteps; in many cases we
clearly ought not to. Should Percy Bysshe Shelley have
modelled himself on Sir Timothy? Evidently the father

that we ought to follow is the intuitive conscience, the divine spark, however small, that we come to recognize through knowledge of ourselves.

Matthew Arnold has been referred to, explicitly or implicitly, several times in the course of this review, and it is borne in upon one, that however much Mr. Eliot may quarrel with Arnold, he is his successor, indeed his close descendant. He is, in fact, the Arnold of our day; and though he is a greater poet—which is saying a great deal— it may be doubted whether he is so good, so general a moralist, perhaps because he is not so clear (some might say, so irritatingly insistent). But then he is trying to do, at the same time, two extremely difficult things: the first, to gain acceptance for a morality to which in 1953 most people will be refractory; the second, to create a new kind of play, new in the form used as vehicle for an idea, new in the way the impact on the audience is effected. This is admirable. Pick at it as we may among ourselves as men of letters, as men of letters we should stoutly support the valiant originality. Mr. Eliot may not be the Shakespeare of our time: but perhaps, in the revival of poetic drama that he is eager to see, he is, as he hopes, the Kyd or Tourneur or Marlowe, which after all is a very splendid position to hold.

THE ELDER STATESMAN

WHAT most critics of Mr. Eliot's plays seem to ignore is that he is writing a new kind of drama. Whereas most plays appeal to the passions—pity, terror, the glamour of love—or to the intellect, or would stir our zeal for political reform, his plays are based on an appeal to the conscience, or the consciousness of self. Here is this person, he says in effect, guilty of this or that; how far are you, dear spectator, in the like case? Our response comes from a different centre. That is why some people do not applaud his plays; nobody likes to be made to think about his weakness, his failures, or his sins. Not that many of us have committed crimes: but then crimes, as we are told in this play, are in relation to the law, sins in relation to the sinner. To be sure, plays *about* conscience are not lacking; we need only think of *Hamlet*, or of *Julius Caesar*, or, for that matter, the Oedipus plays. *The Elder Statesman*, indeed, has a close relation to these last; there is a possible accidental murder, a mortifying sexual business, which worry Lord Claverton's conscience, and a final reconciliation as at Colonus, a kind of redemption. *Oedipus at Colonus* is only a shadowy background, 'a starting-point', to use Mr. Eliot's own phrase for what he owes the classical drama; the background does not obtrude. But in all the plays about conscience, from Sophocles to Ibsen, we are detached spectators. We sympathize with the struggling character, we perhaps enter into his difficulties, his agonies. Here, however, we are forced to ask ourselves: 'Have I never run away from myself? Have I never tried to blot out incidents from my past?'

When we first see Lord Claverton it is as a successful man, though now about to go to a hospital-hotel for a rest cure—he has had a stroke—a man lovingly cherished by his daughter Monica, whom he loves in return, but selfishly, grudging the time she gives to a possible *prétendant*, Charles Hemington. He has had a certain success as a politician, achieving a minor ministry, from which he has retired to become a Chairman of companies in the City, his reputation so growing as to result in his elevation to the House of Lords. All would seem to be well. But then he has a visitor, a hideous reminder of a past that he has admirably managed to consign to oblivion. This is Federico Gomez, a highly successful business man from the Central American Republic of San Marco, a friend from undergraduate days at Oxford. At that time, twenty-five years ago, Claverton was plain Ferry, adopting the hyphen of Claverton-Ferry on his marriage, to lose the Ferry completely when he became a peer. Gomez, whom Claverton does not at first recognize, has also changed his name. In their early days he was Frederick Culverwell; but having been imprisoned for forgery, and then emigrated, he naturally preferred to hide his identity by taking his wife's name on his marriage—a parallel brought out with delicious irony. If, Gomez asks Claverton, Fred Culverwell had changed his name to conceal himself from the world, hadn't Ferry changed his to conceal himself—from whom? himself perhaps?

This meeting is a terrible shock for Claverton, for it leads to the awakening of two skeletons in his cupboard. Exactly what they are is developed only in the course of the play, a kind of Ibsenic back-unfolding. Which is the more humiliating, nagging, or painful to Claverton, even he would be unable to say. The first re-evocation is of an evening when, driving back to Oxford after a spree with Fred and two girls of the light variety, Ferry had run over an old man lying in the road, and *had not stopped*, largely from fear of the authorities knowing about the girls. A little later a lorry-driver had run over the same man, *had* stopped, and would have been tried for manslaughter but that medical evidence proved that the man had died from natural causes before being run over. All through life Claverton hears a voice—it is Culverwell's—saying, 'But you *didn't* stop!' He had run away. And then, secondly, how far was Claverton responsible for Culverwell's downfall by making him, a poor scholarship boy, acquire the tastes of a rich man? Paying for his passage to America hardly cancelled the sin.

The first act leaves us with this much knowledge, and the next gives us, in an aura of comedy, a good deal more. At the rest-home, Claverton is getting a modicum of release, a sense of contentment, ruffled only by the garrulous 'hostess' who pesters him (seeing who he is) by explaining at great length how she always leaves her guests alone, meanwhile cossetting him with rugs and tea. But then he is confronted by another 'patient', a Mrs. Carghill. He doesn't recognize her any more than he had Gomez; but she is a woman whose first lover he had been in his early days; she had brought a breach of promise action against him, resolved out of court for huge sums paid by his father. That episode also has been buried; but was he responsible for the notorious life she had afterwards led in revue? Has his life been nothing but evasion and running away, of which his abandonment of politics was but a symbol, since there he feared failure?

So what is he to do? Here are these two *revenants* blackmailing him, not for money, for both have plenty of that, but for something of himself. Gomez wants his companionship, a renewal of his old friendship. He desperately hankers after a return into English life, to feel again what it is like to be an Englishman in England. Homesickness, he calls it. Mrs. Carghill yearns, in her shallow way, for something of the old closeness. She proposes to read him his long-forgotten love-letters to her, of which she keeps photostat copies always with her, the originals being in her lawyer's strong-box. Claverton is tortured. He has nothing but his daughter's affection, which threatens to be divided by the love of a son-in-law. His own son hates him, rebelling against conformity with his father's wishes for his career, scenting the falsity of all that his father seemingly stands for. The situation is intolerable, but it is resolved in the last part of the third act. Claverton confesses to Monica and Charles, feels the peace that ensues upon confession, and for the first time in his life has 'the illumination of knowing what love is'.

All of us, no doubt, in one degree or another, try to evade the actuality that is ourselves. 'The great business of his life (Dr. Johnson said) was to escape from himself,' so Boswell informs us. But what in a play makes a commonplace theme into a universal one is the power with which it is driven home, how far it is thrown into relief against the whiffling activity, or the pompous pretensions, of everyday life. It is through the gradual revelation of Lord Claverton to himself that Mr. Eliot makes the theme tell. Little by little we hear of Claverton's terror of being alone, and his equal need for privacy; of his loneliness, as he conceives it, his isolation. Isolation? 'You were not isolated,' Culverwell-Gomez tells him brutally; 'you were insulated,' jibing at him too for his conscience, a matter men are seldom heard to mention except to state that it is clear. Little by little Claverton comes to a realization of this covering-up process, which began with a dissatisfaction with himself that made him always seek justification. There is general comment upon the worst failures, that of men who have to pretend to themselves that their failures are successes. He forces himself to admit, 'All the time I've wanted to escape from myself': but you can't escape from your own failures. As the play progresses, and he has every shred of self-respect torn from him, he seems to grow in stature because at last he faces himself. He can even take blows with equanimity. When Mrs. Carghill goes over their broken love-affair, she says that her friend (a mysterious, worldly-shrewd Effie) has told her, 'That man is hollow—or did she say yellow?'; he hardly flinches. It is all part of the accusation he is levelling at himself.

How far his failures haunt him is revealed in the intensely dramatic scene where his son Michael turns upon him and rends him for trying to distort his life. The young man wants to go abroad, to work out his own destiny as an individual, and not dwindle to being the son of a distinguished figure. Why does he want to go abroad? his father asks him. Has he been guilty of manslaughter? Oh no, Michael tells him; he's far too good a driver for that! Has he got into a mess with a woman? 'I'm not such a fool as to get myself involved in a breach of promise case.' He accuses him of wanting to escape, from himself, from his failure in England, the irony of the imputations escaping Michael. Other ironies in the final scene do not escape him, as when Gomez with sly malice claims that in paying Michael's passage to San Marco, and proposing to act there as his guide in life, he is repaying Ferry for what he did for Culverwell, as his guide, all too easy philosopher, and hasty benefactor.

If the first two acts are dramatic enough in their surprises, the play in the last, moving scene becomes contemplative rather than dramatic, unity being maintained by the thread of comedy, not always ironic, which Mr. Eliot skilfully weaves into the basic sadness surrounding the man we now know to be dying, and who comes to know it himself, not without relief. 'It is worth while dying, to find out what life is.' At the end he achieves tremendous dignity. When he tells Monica and Charles that he is going to confess, he asks Charles if there is nothing in his life he would wish to hide, some meanness, cowardice, or even occasion for ridicule? Here, of course, he touches all of us. 'We are the hollow men, We are the stuffed men' just as much as he is. But can he be honest, even at this point? when he has spent all his life trying to cover himself up, from himself as much as from the world? Can he face reality? Monica helps him. These dreadful people, Gomez and Mrs. Carghill, are not real; they are ghosts that can be exorcized. We have all to face our own ghosts. And he comes to realize that he has never yet been able to confess because he has passed his life without love, even for his wife, and you cannot confess if you are sure of the wrong response. And does Monica love him, the real him, or only an idol, the part he plays, the sham he has built up? She responds beautifully; her love for Charles has given her understanding: and Claverton's love also enlarges itself. From being selfish and possessive—though, as he says, we must always respect love whenever we meet it, however selfish it may be—it becomes generous; he gladly gives Monica to Charles, and she comes to love her father with a more real love now that she sees him for what he really is. Love, in fact, is the resolution of the whole play, which at the end is suffused with an ethos that is a curious dovetailing of the Christian ethos with that of the Perennial Philosophy. 'I am only a beginner in love,' the stricken man says; 'but that is something.' He professes love even for his son, in a passage that comes perilously near the sentimental. Yet his extraordinary new dignity asserts itself as he withdraws to meditate under the beech tree, a place which has become to him a kind of holy spot.

This has been called, and is now advertised on the posters as being, 'Mr. Eliot's most human play'. This may be because of the delicacy with which he treats the young lovers, but one ventures to think that it is judged to be such because of its greater clarity. Not that the story is plainer than in, say, The Confidential Clerk, but that the phrasing is absolutely sure throughout. There is never a word wasted. It is written in Mr. Eliot's own form of verse, though only once or twice does it have the rhythm or intensity of poetry; but then, verse on the stage is no more than the most effective form of speech for an actor to utter. The structure of the play too is beautifully balanced, dramatic structure being the way in which the emotions are induced in the spectator to produce a final result. There is no dominant crisis, either in the action or emotionally; there is a kind of inexorable movement from the beginning. It might be accounted to fail dramatically as a whole, though not in detail. Yet, after all, one judges a play by the mood in which one leaves the theatre. Has the katharsis (or whatever you like to call it) appropriate to the kind of play been achieved? Has it enlarged the bounds of one's sympathy with or understanding of other people? or in this case, has it brought about any kind of revelation of one's self to one's self? Judged by such standards, *The Elder Statesman* is Mr. Eliot's best play of the peculiar individual kind he has set himself to fashion, enduing a popular form with a deeper meaning.

Best, of course, within its particular context, and measured by the degree to which the dramatist has succeeded in doing what he set out to do, provided always that the 'matter' was worth dramatization. It has been complained, and so far as that goes the young couple in the play urge it upon Claverton, that to let conscience over errors prey upon one to the extent depicted, is morbid; errors moreover that have produced no harm. (Incidentally Claverton comments that but for his running away neither Gomez nor Mrs. Carghill would have been so triumphantly successful in life; the one would have become a grammar-school master, the other led a life of incompatibility with a man condemned to poverty by his father.) Morbid? Maybe. But without conscience no civilized community is possible; and it is the business of the dramatist to isolate and underline certain characteristics in human behaviour. The play lacks, perhaps, the pitying humanity of *Murder in the Cathedral*; no characters emerge so starkly and yet so subtly as Agatha and Lady Monchensey in *The Family Reunion*; and so on with the other plays. But from all the previous plays the spectator, I do not say the reader, emerges with a certain puzzledom. All draw their response from the individual conscience, in varying degrees; but the moral problem posed does not seem to find its solution completely in the action of the characters, or if it does, it is based on premises not all can accept. There is loss and gain; but it would seem, immediately after seeing it, that although something has been lost from the giddier round-abouts of the earlier plays, more has been gained on the simpler swings of the present one.

LAWRENCE DURRELL

THE ALEXANDRIAN SERIES

INCONTESTABLY, Lawrence Durrell is a man of remarkable talents. Moreover, everything that he writes is distinguished by a rich, sensuous appreciation of language, a capacity for vivid adventurous imagery, and a feeling for the modulation of phrase. That is, he is above all things 'a writer'; words mean something to him as though they had a tactile actuality, corresponding with the thing described. His poem 'Style' may illuminate his procedure, half-will, half-abandonment:

> Something like the sea,
> Unlaboured momentum of water.
> But going somewhere,
> Building and subsiding,
> The busy one, the loveless.
>
> Or the wind that slits
> Forests from end to end,
> Inspiriting vast audiences,
> Ovations of leafy hands
> Accepting, accepting.
>
> But neither is yet
> Fine enough for the line I hunt
> The dry bony blade of the
> Sword-grass might suit me
> Better: an assassin of polish. . . .

(The Tree of Idleness)

1 *Justine* (1957); *Balthazar* (1958); *Mountolive* (1958); *Clea* (1960). London: Faber and Faber. New York: E. P. Dutton and Co.; Referred to in the text by their initials.

If, often, we are carried away by the seemingly un-laboured momentum of his style, a varied buoyant surge (not always free of spray), the dry bony blade occasionally cuts through effectively. His descriptions of Alexandria and the surrounding country that, you might say, 'para-graph' these volumes are such that we 'see' in the way he describes in one of his travel-books:

> But it was not a view that one 'saw' in the strict sense; it radiated over one, dancing in that brown heat, pouring into the eyes and spreading with the five senses—as light enters the pin-hole of a camera's lens but floods the whole gelatine surface of the negative.
>
> *(Reflections on a Marine Venus)*

Nor is it of actual landscapes alone that he gives us the sense; often it is of people in action within the landscapes, as in the virtuoso action-pictures of duck-shooting on Lake Mareotis (J. 210 *seq*:), or the fishing (M. 11 *seq*:), where human noise and conflict are mingled with the noisy and conflicting nature. Or there are the purely human scenes, quiet, perhaps, as when the blind sheikh recites the *suras* to an enraptured group of corrupt men of affairs (M. 265); or clangorous as when crowds gather to honour the shrine of the scandalous transvestist Englishman, Scobie, fantastic-ally become a Moslem saint, El Scob, of which a small part of the kaleidoscopic scene may serve as a taste.

> And as the chanters move forward to recite the holy texts, six Mevlevi dervishes suddenly took the centre of the stage, expanding in a slow fan of movement until they had formed a semicircle. They wore brilliant white robes reaching to their green slippered feet and tall brown hats shaped like huge *bombes glacées*. Calmly, beautifully, they began to whirl, these 'tops spun by God', while the music of the flutes haunted them with their piercing quibbles. As they gathered momentum their arms, which at first they hugged fast to their shoulders, unfolded as if by centrifugal force and stretched out to full reach, the right palm turned upward to heaven, the left downward to the ground. So, with heads and tall rounded hats tilted slightly, like the axis of the earth, they stayed there

miraculously spinning, their feet hardly seeming to touch the floor, in this wonderful parody of the heavenly bodies in their perpetual motion. (C. 269)

Such is the décor, compellingly effective, capturing the reader, within which the characters, varied, subtle, only occasionally admirable, perform gyrations comparable with those of the dancing dervishes.

This whirling movement is not altogether due to the characters themselves, for this glamour is only part of the method Mr. Durrell uses for giving us a vision of his people. His great originality consists in his extreme endeavour to abolish the common illusion of time, and he gradually reveals his perilous exploration. 'What I most need to do is to record experiences, not in the order in which they took place—for that is history—but in the order in which they became significant for me.' (J. 115) This is a little to ignore the danger, for, as St. Augustine said, 'Times lose no time: nor do they idly go and return about these senses of ours; but they cause strange operations in our minds.' Mr. Durrell, however, contends that his time scheme is based on the relativity proposition, relativity being a concept that has long held his imagination, as we see from his highly interesting critical work, *A Key to Modern Poetry* (Peter Nevill, 1952). Thus in the 'Workpoints' at the end of *Justine* we find comments on 'the "n-dimensional novel" trilogy':

> The narrative momentum forward is counter-sprung by references backward in time, giving the impression of a book which is not travelling from A to B but standing above time and turning on its axis to comprehend the whole pattern.

The whole theory is set out more fully, indeed, as Mr. Durrell himself suggests, a little pompously, in the Note prefacing *Balthazar*.

Three sides of space and one of time constitute the soup-mix recipe of a continuum. The four novels follow this pattern.

The three first parts, however, are to be deployed spatially . . . and are not linked in serial form. They interlap, interweave, in a purely spatial relation. Time is stayed. The fourth part alone will represent time, and be a true sequel.

The subject-object relation is so important to relativity that I have tried to turn the novel through both subjective and objective models.

Later in this volume we are told by Pursewarden, a novelist and poet of genius, we are given to understand, who throughout seems to speak as Mr. Durrell's *alter ego*, that 'the Relativity proposition was directly responsible for abstract painting, atonal music, and formless (or at any rate cyclic forms in) literature'. (B. 142) And finally we read of 'passing a common axis through four stories, say . . . a continuum . . . embodying not a *temps retrouvé* but a *temps délivré*.' (C. 135) That is, illustrating 'Space-Time' and not Bergsonian 'Duration', which latter is the method of Proust or Joyce. (B. Note)

Thus *Justine*, written by Darley (who has the same initials as Mr. Durrell, L. G. D., enabling Pursewarden to nickname him Lineaments of Gratified Desire, 'Lineaments' for short), autobiographically relates certain events. *Balthazar* covers the same events, again related by Darley, but heavily annotated by Balthazar—'interlineations' they are called—giving a markedly different impression of the same events and characters. *Mountolive*, 'objectively' written, covers the same time, but gives different prominence to the characters, acting in different spheres, besides introducing a political background. *Clea*, again by Darley, carries the story forward with such characters as are still alive, but also looks back a good deal. Each volume concludes with a series of 'Workpoints', full of suggestions, of ideas not worked out, or which Mr. Durrell has not been able to fit into his pattern. (Given the speed at which these books were written, it is not surprising that such scraps should fly off the whirling structure.)

It sounds chaotic, but in the event the result is often extremely effective. The object is very largely achieved of giving the reader the same sort of impact made by events, with all their colourings of the past and hopes of the future, as actually lived and experienced. Moreover we get the 'prismatic' view of character that Mr. Durrell aims at, carrying out the idea that Justine propounded to Darley as she sat before the multiple mirrors at her dressmaker's: 'Now if I wrote I would try for a multi-dimensional effect in character, a sort of prism-sightedness. Why should not people show more than one profile at a time?' (J. 27) There is perhaps nothing very new in this last idea: Henry James did much the same with his 'strings'. But by combining the methods, matters, or doings which seemed mysterious or incomprehensible in *Justine*, such as Justine's sudden disappearance to Palestine, are cleared up in the later works. Even so not altogether; different mirrors have different emotions, as well as varying points of view, as we are to gather from a quotation from de Sade which provides an epigraph to *Balthazar*:

> The mirror sees the man as beautiful, the mirror loves the man; another mirror sees the man as frightful and hates him; and it is always the same being who produces the impression.

Thus the explanation of an event varies. Take, for instance, Pursewarden's suicide, incomprehensible in *Justine*, in *Mountolive* the result of an irresolvable conflict between duty and affection (M. 234), but seen in *Clea* as a willing self-sacrifice for the sister whom he incestuously loved.

All this constitutes a freshly effective method for unravelling the subtle intricacies of character, especially where the character is complex, as in the case of Justine herself, who loves, one might say, indiscriminately, but never completely, always looking for something else. We learn of her early life from another narrator, Arnauti, her first husband (hardly touched on in this work), whose novel, *Moeurs*, is generally supposed to be an account of his marriage with Justine. Here, her inability to love wholly, her 'check', is ascribed to her having been raped as a child. After the divorce of this couple, Justine leads a promiscuous life, that of the old Alexandrian hetaira, until (although she is a Jewess) she is sought in marriage by Nessim Hosnani, a rich Coptic landlord and business man. Nessim loves her, yes; but her feeling for him is one of respect and admiration rather than love. She does not quite understand his first approaches:

'. . . What can I do about not loving you?'
'You must, of course, never try to.'
'Then what sort of life could we make?'
Nessim looked at her with hot shy eyes and then lowered his glance to the table, as if under a cruel rebuke. 'Tell me,' she said after a silence, 'Please tell me. I cannot use your fortune and your position and give you nothing in exchange, Nessim.'
'If you would care to try,' he said gently, 'we need not delude each other. Life isn't very long. One owes it to oneself to try to find a means to happiness.'
'Is it that you want to sleep with me?' asked Justine suddenly: disgusted yet touched beyond measure by his tone. 'You may. Yes. O! I would do anything for you, Nessim—anything.'
But he flinched and said: 'I am speaking about an understanding in which friendship and knowledge can take the place of love until and if it comes as I hope. Of course I shall sleep with you— myself a lover, and you a friend. Who knows? In a year, perhaps. All Alexandrian marriages are business ventures after all. My God, Justine, what a fool you are. Can't you see that we might possibly need each other without fully realising it? It's worth trying. Everything may stand in the way. But I can't get over the thought that in the whole city the woman I most *need* is you.' (B. 60)

The whole passage of a few pages is of concentrated interest; and all through the series we get different 'prismatic' views of the marriage, as when Nessim tells

Clea (M. 195) that he knows all about Justine's sad, mad, bad past, but that she would match perfectly his own—the word is intended to come as a surprise—*aridity*. Or was it perhaps a political alliance, the Copt and the Jewess allying themselves for the anti-Arab plot which causes such misery to them all? 'They make a perfect pair, but never seem to touch each other.' (M. 110) They certainly make an outwardly perfect pair in Darley's eyes in *Justine*, but soon we get the strange business of her affair with him. As they are lying side by side on a beach after bathing, the idea of love came into their minds.

> If I said now: 'It must not happen to us,' she must have replied: 'But let us *suppose*. What if it did?' Then—and this I remember clearly—the mania for self-justification seized her . . . and between those breathless half-seconds when I felt her strong mouth on my own and those worldly brown arms closing upon mine: 'I would not mistake it for gluttony or self-indulgence. We are too worldly for that: simply we have something to learn from each other. What is it? . . .'
> 'I do not know,' she said with a savage, obstinate, desperate expression of humility upon her face. 'I do not know': and she pressed herself upon me like someone pressing upon a bruise. It was as if she wished to expunge the very thought of me, and yet in the fragile quivering context of every kiss found a sort of painful surcease—like cold water on a sprain. How well I recognized her now as a child of the city, which decrees that its women shall be the voluptuaries not of pleasure but of pain, doomed to hunt for what they least dare to find. (J. 47)

And as they walked away:

> She was in a towering rage. 'You thought I simply wanted to make love? God! haven't we had enough of that? How is it that you do not *know* what I feel for once? How is it? . . . After all,' I remember her saying, 'this has nothing to do with sex.' (J. 48)

They do not meet for a little time, then one day she appears at the flat that Darley inhabits with his mistress, Melissa, and insists on going to bed with him: 'I want to put an end to all this as soon as possible. I feel we've gone too far to go back.' (J. 84) But yet, according to Balthazar's 'interlineation', all this was but a cloak to hide from Nessim the passion she felt for Pursewarden, who obliges, but mockingly. No wonder she could remark: 'We use each other like axes to cut down the ones we really love.' (J. 112)

Apart from her love-affairs and her political concerns, Justine is haunted by the agonized feeling she has for the daughter—whom she had by her marriage with Arnauti—that was stolen and probably taken to a child-brothel. It most likely died; there are two versions of this. Justine was forever searching for her daughter.

> I found it, of course . . . in a brothel. It died from something, perhaps meningitis. Darley and Nessim came and dragged me away. All of a sudden I realized that I could not bear to find it: all the time I hunted I lived on the hope of finding it. But this thing, once dead, seemed to deprive me of all purpose. I recognized it, but my inner mind kept crying out that it was not true, refusing to let me recognize it, even though I had already consciously done so. (C. 144)

A complex tangle of emotions which Pursewarden, who admired her with reservations, seeing in her 'the configurations of an unhappiness that was genuine, though it always smelt of greasepaint', comments on in considerable detail. (C. 145)

These are merely samples of a character that must be admitted to be extremely intricate, and which the 'prismatic' method brings out in amazing relief. Whether it is entirely convincing is another matter. The same is largely true of some ten of the other personages in the series, who are treated in this way—though not at the same length; and there are some subsidiary characters sketched in simply and objectively, though not always understandingly, such as Maskelyne, the soldier seconded for intelligence duties. Thus the main characters are fascinatingly and surprisingly

12

glossed. Nessim, for example, outwardly the successful business man, the munificent host; another part of him devoted to the Coptic plot; yet another dreaming obsessedly about Alexandrian history. Or Narouz, his brother, as one mirror sees him a charming, purely country person, vowed to agriculture and horsemanship, filled with warm family feelings; as another mirror sees him hideously sadistic, and a murderer; brutally physical in his desires, yet a mystic who can address a Coptic meeting with all the fervour and rapt conviction of a religious prophet, politically so dangerous that his brother, who is devoted to him, has to have him killed. Then again there is Balthazar, the pederastic doctor, who holds meetings, which most of the main characters attend, for the discussion of the Hermetic philosophy. The women also are intricately presented: Leila, the mother of Nessim and Narouz, who, at the instigation of her paralytic husband (capable, incidentally, of a moving tirade about the historical importance of, and the wrongs suffered by, the Copts [M. 40 seq.]) takes the young English diplomat, Mountolive, as a lover, educates him by letters when he goes back to Europe, but for various reasons refuses to meet him when he returns to Egypt as the first British ambassador. There is Clea, whose passionate aim in life is to be a painter: and finally Melissa, the cabaret prostitute, a touching figure, devoted and tender, alone among the whole cast requiring nothing for herself.

But there is one thing that unites all the characters, large or small, in one common bond, and that is a complete lack of sexual continence, even, one might think, of selection. All the men seem to have relations with whores, and apart from that, Darley lives with Melissa while he is having his affair with Justine, and finally sleeps with Clea. Pursewarden seems promiscuous, but loves his sister, who finally loves Mountolive, yet does not mind—that is the right phrase—sleeping with Justine. Or there is the tragi-comic Scobie, with his predilection for black boys; Pombal, a haunter of brothels, who is momentarily 'entrapped' by a real love, but when his lover is killed, reverts to promiscuity. Prominent is the shameless lecher Capodistria, who is, however, also interested in black magic. Mountolive is Leila's lover, has a child by a ballet dancer, but finally loves Pursewarden's sister. Clea, having first loved Justine, is passionate for a certain Amaril, but then succumbs to Darley. What is it that drives all these people? It is not mere pleasure-seeking.

For something drives them, and here Mr. Durrell leads us to the psychology of Groddeck, always of interest to him, as we learn from *A Key to Modern Poetry*, 'because his equating of mind and body does in the medical field, what Einstein has done in the realm of physics with the concepts of space and time'. He quotes from Groddeck: 'I assume that man is animated by the It which directs what he does and what he goes through, and that the assertion "I live" only expresses a small and superficial part of the total experience "I am lived by the It" '. This story about the inhabitants of Alexandria is therefore a portrait of Alexandria, which 'lives' the characters. This is variously stated several times:

I see all of us not as men and women any longer, identities swollen with their acts of forgetfulness, follies, and deceits—but as beings unconsciously made part of place, buried to the waist among the ruins of a single city, steeped in its values. (B. 225)

We are the children of our landscape; it dictates behaviour and even thought in the measure to which we are responsive to it. (J. 41)

It is a strange and kaleidoscopic Alexandria that lives these people, a place of overwhelming beauty as of hideous sordor, with a history going back to before Alexander, with its extraordinary mixture of 'five races, five languages, a dozen creeds', (J. 14) with Antony and Cleopatra, with

the saints and mystics, the armies and traders, the one
living representative of the place 'the old poet', to wit
C. P. Cavafy, phrases from whose poems are quoted in the
text, some pieces being translated in appendixes. Some of
the characters are deeply conscious of the spirit of the
place, especially Nessim, who, at a period of almost
madness, in imagination lives scenes of past centuries.

At this time he had already begun to experience that great cycle
of historical dreams which now replaced the dreams of childhood in
his mind, and into which the City now threw itself—as if at last it
had found a responsive subject through which to express the collective desires, the collective wishes, which informed its culture.
He would wake to see the towers and minarets printed on the
exhausted, dust-powdered sky, and see as if *en montage* on them the
giant footprints of the historical memory which lies behind the
recollections of individual personality, its mentor and guide: indeed
its inventor, since man is only an extension of the spirit of place.
(J. 175)

Most significant is that it should be a place where
'sexual provender lies to hand in staggering variety and
profusion', and is 'the great wine-press of love'.   (J. 14)
Significant, since the series, within its experimental
form, has as its 'central topic', we are told in the prefatory
note to *Balthazar*, 'an investigation of modern love'.
Modern?   As old, one might suggest, as Alexandria itself.
But let us look at some of the *obiter dicta* on love scattered
throughout these volumes.   Talking of what love means to
her, Justine explains:

The doctor I loved told me I was a nymphomaniac—but there is no
gluttony or self-indulgence in my pleasure . . . You speak of taking
pleasure sadly, like the puritans do . . . I take it tragically.   (J. 68)

Clea talks to Darley about his love for Justine:

. . . the love you now feel for Justine is not a different love for a
different object but the same love you feel for Melissa trying to work
itself out through the medium of Justine.   Love is horribly stable,

and each of us is only allotted a certain portion of it, a ration. It is capable of appearing in an infinity of forms and attaching itself to an infinity of people. But it is limited in quantity, can be used up, become shop-worn and faded before it reaches its true object. (J. 130)

Pursewarden is reported to have said:

I believe that Gods are men, and men Gods; they intrude on each other's lives, trying to express themselves through each other . . . I think that very few people realize that sex is a psychic and not a physical act. (B. 124)

And he writes:

At first we seek to supplement the emptiness of our individuality through love, and for a brief moment enjoy the illusion of completeness. (B. 234)

It is a relief to find Clea reporting him as saying 'English has two great forgotten words, namely "helpmeet" which is much greater than "lover", and "loving-kindness" which is so much greater than "love", or even "passion" '.

He supports his flauntingly frank exposition of completely amoral sexual life, already amply covered in his Henry Millerish *The Black Book* (not to be purchased in England), by offering an extract from de Sade as an epigraph to each volume, following Pursewarden's example, who did so, he said:

Because he demonstrates pure rationalism—the ages of sweet reason we have lived through since Descartes. He is the final flower of reason, and the typic of European behaviour. (B. 247)

Pursewarden unrelentingly attacks English prudery, the Anglo-Saxons at the bottom of whose soul 'there is a still small voice forever whispering "Is this Quaite Naice?" '. (B. 247) He urges that we should 'come to terms with our own human obscenity', (M. 65) whereas Darley asks whether 'obscene' is not 'surely the stupidest word in our language'. (C. 260) Every sensibly honest man comes to terms with his own obscenity; but need he, we ask, revel in it to quite the extent that the persons in this book do? Man, it may be conceded, is basically an animal, a sexual animal; but that is not the most interesting thing about him. Obscenity, as Katherine Anne Porter said recently in a discussion of *Lady Chatterley's Lover*, 'is real, is necessary as expression, a safety-valve against the almost intolerable pressures and strains of relationship between men and women, and not only between men and women, but between any human being and his unmanageable world'. But with Mr. Durrell it seems almost a principle; it is not good wholesome bawdry which anyone but a prig enjoys; it is as though he were animated by what has been called 'the Freudian piety towards the sinister', which becomes sometimes revolting, even sadistic, as when he describes Clea's embryo child surgically aborted, the mutilation of her hand, the dismemberment of living camels (twice), the use Narouz makes of his whip, or the dwelling upon circumcision.

But it would be giving a totally wrong impression of this series to suggest that all this was the whole, or even the greater part of its interest. There are many themes strung through it, one, which in a sense is the dominating theme, being a discussion of the literary art, more especially of novel-writing. These come largely through Pursewarden, his direct comments, his remarks as reported by others, quotations from his books, and, most important, his lengthy 'Conversations with Brother Ass' (C. 125-154), Brother Ass being his fellow-novelist Darley. All his utterances need not be given the same importance; many of them are conversational gambits, the trying out of ideas, casual comments over drinks in a bar, such as any author may emit from time to time. They are often what might be called 'confessions of a writer', one trying to be rigorously honest. Others also comment. The solace of a work of art, Darley tells us, 'lies in this—that only *there*, in the silences of the painter or the writer can reality be reordered, reworked, and made to show its significant side'. (J. 17) Balthazar tells us that the artist is a person who has 'the temerity to try to impose a pattern upon [life] which he infects with his own meanings'. (B. 175) Darley tries to 'match the truth to the illusions which are necessary to art without the gap showing'. (C. 72); 'Music,' Clea once remarked, 'was invented to confirm human loneliness.' (C. 65) Solitude, indeed, is another theme that occasionally haunts these pages, mingled with that of love. 'One makes love,' Pursewarden tells us, 'only to confirm one's loneliness.' (C. 64) When dancing at a cabaret with Melissa he asks her, *Comment vous défendez-vous contre la solitude?*, she answers, *Monsieur, je suis devenue la solitude même.* (J. 201 and M. 167) Other notions continually crop up, such as the power of the imagination—and others to be touched on later—all woven into the general texture of the whole, in conversation, or as pregnant asides. In fact it is an extraordinarily rich tapestry that Mr. Durrell displays; every page is a stimulus to the mind or the visual sense. There are plenty of things to dislike in the quartet, as well as to rejoice in; but there is no doubt that as one reads one is swept away, absorbed, with a sense that life and people are continually being revealed, that one's knowledge is being added to.

As one reads, yes: but what when one comes to consider? For what can we derive from this glimpse of pullulating humanity, this muck and brothel dominated background, with these people on the whole will-less, 'gorged by introspection', allowing themselves to be lived Groddeck-wise by a ravenous and dissatisfied It? However much we may allow for 'the heraldic aspect of reality',

(C. 137 and 153) we cannot but agree with Pursewarden when he says to Brother Ass:

And here we are both in a foreign city built upon smegma-tinted crystal and tinsel whose *moeurs*, if we described them, would be regarded as the fantasies of our disordered brains.   (C. 130)

For these people for the most part have no sense of values. 'I want to learn to respect nothing, while despising nothing,' Pursewarden exclaims.   (M. 65) 'All ideas seem equally good to me,' Darley declares; 'the fact of their existence proves that someone is creating.   Does it matter whether they are objectively right or wrong?'   (J. 41) Much in the same vein Arnauti tells us about his relations with Justine: 'Strangely enough it was never in the *lover* that I met her, but in the *writer*.   Here we clasped hands —in that amoral world of suspended judgements where curiosity and wonder seem greater than order—the syllogistic order imposed by the mind.'   (J. 72)

For whom in these volumes can we feel admiration, or even respect?   Which of these people has any trace of nobility, even of that self-discipline without which the bonds of society are loosed?   Among the women, Clea, in her will to paint, claims some regard, and Leila, the Coptic materfamilias, in her care for Mountolive's intellectual health and in her love for her son Nessim, is a person one can respect.   Among those men who figure as main characters it is only Mountolive and Nessim that we can at all, in some degree, admire;   and it is to be noted that when Mountolive met Nessim for the first time he 'instantly recognized in him a person of his own kind, a person whose life was a code'.   (M. 26)   A pleasant meeting for us also, after companioning with amoral people in whom there is no real central conflict, and so no really dramatic being.

Religion, except for fanatical varieties, hardly enters into the picture.   Justine, perhaps, makes the nearest approach to a religious sense, when she writes, or so Nessim records:

While I respect your discipline and your knowledge I feel that if I am ever going to come to terms with myself I must work *through* the dross in my own character and burn it up. Anyone could solve my problem artificially by placing it in the lap of a priest. We Alexandrians have more pride than that—and more respect for religion. It would not be fair to God, my dear sir, and whoever else I fail (I see you smile) I am determined not to fail Him whoever He is. (J. 72-3)

The reader also, when he knows Justine, may smile, as he may at Pursewarden's courage: 'it is with God we must be the most careful; for He makes such a powerful appeal to what is *lowest* in human nature—our feelings of insufficiency, fear of the unknown, personal failings. . . .' (J. 140) He prefers to regard God as the supreme Ironist. Yet though, to judge from other writings of his, Mr. Durrell finds the Moslems repugnant, he allows one sound to affect Darley deeply.

In that early spring dawn, with its dense dew, sketched upon the silence which engulfs a whole city before the birds awaken it, I caught the sweet voice of the blind *muezzin* [Mr. Durrell, it seems, prefers his muezzins blind] from the mosque reciting the *Ebed*—a voice hanging like a hair in the palm cooled upper airs of Alexandria. 'I praise the perfection of God, the Forever existing' (this repeated thrice, ever more slowly, in a high sweet register). 'The perfection of God, the Desired, the Existing, the Single, the Supreme: the perfection of God, the One, the Sole: the perfection of Him who taketh unto himself no male or female partner. . . .

The great prayer wound its way into my sleepy consciousness like a serpent, coil after coil of shining words—the voice of the *muezzin* sinking from register to register of gravity—until the whole morning seemed dense with its marvellous healing power, the intimations of a grace undeserved and unexpected.

So in *Justine* (25), repeated almost word for word in *Clea* (99). But, we may note a little cynically, these intimations of a grace undeserved and unexpected come to Darley

after nights of gratified sexual love, on the first occasion
with Melissa, on the second with Clea!

Yet, a little oddly in view of an achieved amoral attitude, the idea of guilt serves as another thread in the
quartet. Liza, talking to Darley about the child born to
her and her brother Pursewarden, which had died, says:

> Her death suddenly made him guilty. Our relationship foundered
> there; and yet it became in another way even more intense, closer.
> We were united by our guilt from that moment. I have often asked
> myself why it should be so. Tremendous unbroken happiness and
> then . . . one day, like an iron shutter falling, *guilt*. (C. 174)

Even Darley can think that 'Guilt always hurries towards its
complement, punishment.' (J. 147) In similar contra-
dictions Pursewarden, for all his rather jeering hardness,
an amorality he seems to work for, is made humane in
another sense by his tenderness. Darley decides, when
talking about him, that,

> underneath all his preoccupations with sex, society, religion, etc.
> (all the staple abstractions which allow the forebrain to chatter)
> there is, quite simply, a man *tortured beyond endurance by the lack of
> tenderness in the world*. (J. 244)

And in describing to Clea what he wants his final novel to
do, Pursewarden writes:

> It should convey some feeling that the world we live in is founded in
> something too simple to be over-described as cosmic law—but as
> easy to grasp as, say, an act of tenderness, simple tenderness in the
> primal relation between animal and plant, rain and soil, seed and
> trees, man and God. A relation so delicate that it is all too easily
> broken by the inquiring mind and *conscience* in the French sense. . . .
> Perhaps the key lies in laughter, in the Humorous God? It is after
> all the serious who disturb the peace of the heart with their antics
> —like Justine. (B. 238, 9)

But what is it that Mr. Durrell wants his novel to do?
What kind of vision of humanity does this work provide?

His object in writing may be, as Pursewarden's was, 'to grow a personality which in the end enables man to transcend art,' (B. 141) but the object of reading, one imagines, is not only to deepen and illumine one's experience of living, however vicariously, but also to adjust, strengthen, and develop one's sense of values, notably, where the novel is concerned, one's social values, those which make society livable. Mr. Durrell has asked in *The Times Literary Supplement*, 27 May 60, 'Can the artist offer no clues to living? Alas, no; his public does that for him.' Surely that is too easy an evasion of responsibility. Not that one would wish for a *prêchis-prêchas*, as M. de Norpois would say, but one asks for clarification. Tchekov, perhaps, put it as well as anybody. There are

two entirely separate things: the solving of a problem and the presentation of that problem correctly. Only the second is the concern of the artist. In *Anna Karenina* or *Eugene Onegin* no problem is resolved, but those works are satisfying, all the same, because the problems are correctly presented.

What problems are presented here? What sense of humanity do the characters give us? They have so far crushed the lees of pain from sanguine grapes of pleasure (to reverse Swinburne's phrase)—in feverish efforts, and by no means at leisure—that for them there is hardly left to drain

> A single sob of pleasure,
> A single pulse of pain.

So what is it that one can feel about them?

On the whole, just pity. 'All great books,' Pursewarden once jotted down, 'are excursions into pity' (M. 166); and these volumes, especially the last, are suffused with this sense. Mr. Durrell has an acute awareness of human misery, and realizes only too poignantly that 'one never knows enough about people and their sufferings to have the right response ready at the moment'. (C. 221)

But is pity enough? Does it suffice just to note the sadness of *la condition humaine* without offering any escape from the depths either of the spirit or the body? What we feel that Mr. Durrell demands of us is a helpless, not a Stoical, acceptance of what at our most feeble we are, a submission without protest to the idea that we are things lived by an It. For the Stoic, though he accepts, does not wholly submit, but realizes that

> unless aboue himself he can
> Erect himselfe, how poore a thing is man!

Perhaps that is the enrichment we shall gain from the splendidly coloured, vivid experience that reading this quartet constitutes. Yet it is an enrichment that would be worth more if we could feel that this is the holdfast Mr. Durrell meant to endow us with. For we might say of this striking experiment what Pursewarden said of Justine: 'Justine and her city are alike in that they both have a strong flavour without having any real character.' (J. 139)

FOR FURTHER READING

Below will be found a short list of works which will extend the scope of what has been said in the foregoing essays. Only complete books dealing with the authors have been included. To have made an extensive bibliography, especially one to include the many admirable critical essays which have appeared in journals, would have meant lists which would only baffle the general reader.

HENRIK IBSEN

The Life of Ibsen. By Halvdan Koht. Trs. by R. L. McMahon and H. A. Larsen. 2 vols. 1931.

Correspondence of Henrik Ibsen. Trs. by Mary Morrison. 1905.

Ibsen. The Intellectual Background. By Brian W. Downs. 1946.

Ibsen the Norwegian. By M. C. Bradbrook. 1946.

Ibsen's Dramatic Technique. By P. F. D. Tennant. 1948.

Ibsen. By G. Wilson Knight. 1962.

THOMAS HARDY

The Life of Thomas Hardy. By Florence Emily Hardy. 1962.

Thomas Hardy. By Lascelles Abercrombie. 1912.

Thomas Hardy's Universe. A Study of a Poet's Mind. By E. Brennecke. 1924.

Thomas Hardy. A Critical Study. By A. S. MacDowell. 1931.

Thomas Hardy. By Edmund Blunden. English Men of
   Letter Series. 1941.
Hardy the Novelist. By Lord David Cecil. 1943.
Hardy. By George D. Wing. 1963.
Thomas Hardy. By R. A. Scott-James. Writers and
   their Work.* 1951.

* These booklets are published by Longmans, Green & Co. for the
British Council and the National Book League. Each contains a
fairly extensive bibliography of the authors treated, with a list of
their works and editions, together with biographies, full length
critical studies, and articles in journals.

RUDYARD KIPLING

Rudyard Kipling. By Edward Shanks. 1940.
Rudyard Kipling. By Hilton Brown. 1945.
Rudyard Kipling. By Rupert Croft-Cooke. 1948.
Rudyard Kipling. His Life and Work. By Charles
   Carrington. 1955. (The standard biography.)
The Art of Rudyard Kipling. By J. M. S. Tompkins.
   1959.
Rudyard Kipling. By Bonamy Dobrée. Writers and
   their Work. 1951.
Aspects of Kipling's Art. By C. A. Bodelsen. 1964.

E. M. FORSTER

The Writings of E. M. Forster. By Rose Macaulay. 1938.
E. M. Forster. A Study. By Lionel Trilling. 1944.
E. M. Forster. By K. W. Gransden. 1961.
E. M. Forster. By Rex Warner. Writers and their
   Work. 1950. Revised ed. by Rex Warner & John
   Morris. 1960.

D. H. LAWRENCE

D. H. Lawrence. By Rebecca West. 1930.

D. H. Lawrence. By Richard Aldington. 1930.

D. H. Lawrence. By Stephen Potter. 1930.

D. H. Lawrence. A Critical Study. By H. Gregory. 1934.

D. H. Lawrence. By Hugh Kingsmill. 1938.

The Life and Works of D. H. Lawrence. By J. A. Moore. 1951.

D. H. Lawrence. By Kenneth Young. Writers and their Work. 1952.

D. H. Lawrence. Novelist. By F. R. Leavis. 1955.

The Dark Sun. A Study of D. H. Lawrence. By Graham Hough. 1956.

T. S. ELIOT

The Achievement of T. S. Eliot. By F. O. Mathiessen. 1935. Enlarged 1947.

T. S. Eliot. A Study of His Writings by Several Hands. Ed. B. Rajan. 1947.

T. S. Eliot. A Symposium for his Sixtieth Birthday. Ed. Richard March and Tambimuttu. 1948.

The Art of T. S. Eliot. By Helen Gardner. 1949.

T. S. Eliot. A Symposium for his Seventieth Birthday. Ed. Neville Braybrooke. 1958.

T. S. Eliot. By M. C. Bradbrook. Writers and their Work. 1950. Revised 1958.

The Poetry of T. S. Eliot. By D. E. S. Maxwell. 1959.

The Plays of T. S. Eliot. By D. E. Jones. 1960.